SOCIALISM M... SENSE

An unfriendly dialogue

By Sean Matgamna

Socialism makes sense

By Sean Matgamna

This book is dedicated to the memory of Cynthia Baldry (1949-1975), Pat Longman (1950-2010), and Fran Broady (1938-2014)

Cover picture: Jeremy Corbyn speaking at a Labour rally soon after the June 2017 general election, in which a left-wing manifesto won a big increase in the Labour vote

Printed by Imprint Digital, Exeter EX5 5HY
ISBN: 978-1-909639-40-9

Second edition, revised, of *Can Socialism Make Sense?* (2016)

Published February 2018 by Workers' Liberty

20E Tower Workshops
Riley Road
London SE1 3DG
020 7394 8923
awl@workersliberty.org
www.workersliberty.org

This work is licensed under the Creative Commons Attribution 2.5 Generic License.
To view a copy of this license, visit: http://creativecommons.org/licenses/by/2.5/
or send a letter to Creative Commons, 444 Castro Street, Suite 900, Mountain View, California, 94041, USA.

Contents

SOCIALISM MAKES SENSE: AN UNFRIENDLY DIALOGUE

Part 1: Capitalism and Socialism
Capitalist Society... 7
The Social Morality of Capitalism...................................... 13
So, What Is Socialism?.. 17
Socialism Is Discredited By Stalinism?.............................. 21

Part 2: Socialism and Human Nature
Human Nature... 29
The National Health Service... 41

Part 3: The Working Class and Socialism
The Working Class.. 47
Working-Class Solidarity 55
Radical Decline of The Working Class? 59

Part 4: Socialism, Democracy, Stalinism
Is It Either Public Ownership or Democracy? 63
Stalinism in History 67
The Russian Revolution, Socialism, and Democracy 75

Part 5: Democracy and Socialism
Is Democracy Central To Socialism?...................................83
The Evolution of Democracy 87
Democracy in British History 95
Democracy in U.S. History 103
Women and Democracy 109
How Secure Is Democracy? 113

Part 6: Capitalism and The "Invading Socialist Society"
The "Invading Socialist Society" 119
Planning: Who Plans? In Whose Interests? 125
Globalisation, Socialism, and Democracy 129

Part 7: What's In It For Me?
The Shit Jobs 133
Capitalism, Inventors, and Future Progress 136
Is There an Ecological Imperative for Socialism? 143
The "Bird In The Hand" 149
And What's In It For Me? 155

WHAT SOCIALISTS DO, AND WHY WE DO IT **165**

Labour

While the ages changed and sped
I was toiling for my bread.
Underneath my sturdy blows
Forests fell and cities rose.
And the hard reluctant soil
Blossomed richly from my toil.

Palaces and temples grand
Wrought I with my cunning hand.
Rich indeed was my reward —
Stunted soul and body scarred
With the marks of scourge and rod.
I, the tiller of the sod

From the cradle to the grave
Shambled through the world — a slave.
Crushed and trampled, beaten, cursed,
Serving best, but served the worst,
Starved and cheated, gouged and spoiled.
Still I builded, still I toiled

Undernourished, underpaid
In the world myself had made.
Up from slavery I rise,
Dreams and wonder in my eyes.
After brutal ages past
Coming to my own at last

I was slave — but I am free!
I was blind — but I can see!
I, the builder, I, the maker,
I, the calm tradition breaker,
Slave and serf and clod no longer,
Know my strength — and who is stronger?

"BB"

Socialism makes sense
An unfriendly dialogue

The means of production belong to the state. But the state, so to speak, "belongs" to the bureaucracy.
    — Leon Trotsky, *The Revolution Betrayed* (1936)

To the cry of the middle class reformers, "make this or that the property of the government", we reply, "yes, in proportion as the workers are ready to make the government their property".
    — James Connolly, *Workers' Republic*, 10 June 1899

I pondered all these things, and how men fight and lose the battle, and the thing that they fought for comes about in spite of their defeat, and when it comes turns out not to be what they meant, and other men have to fight for what they meant under another name...
    — William Morris, *A Dream of John Ball*

Picturehouse cinema workers on strike, London 2017

The Unite union in New Zealand, led by socialists, above, has organised all the main fast food chains, and in 2017 won a ban on zero hours contracts. Also in 2017, cleaners at the London School of Economics (below) won demands to have their contract taken in-house, as well as other gains.

A is a Marxist socialist. B believes that the history of Stalinist Russia and similar systems elsewhere damns socialism, and that capitalism is the only workable social system.

Part 1: Capitalism and socialism

Capitalist society

B. OK, capitalism is imperfect, but it works and gives scope for improvements. Why should anyone with sense want to disrupt it for the sake of your dubious alternatives?

A. The world in which we live is plagued by local wars, by famine and malnutrition in Africa and elsewhere, by ecological disasters now and the certainty of even worse ecological disasters to come. By the "routine" death of about eight million children under the age of five, each year, from preventable or curable diseases.

It is a senselessly class-ridden world. Workers, to live, have to sell their labour-power to an exploitative employer, if they can find one. A moneyed elite owns and controls the means of production, communication, and exchange.

In the USA, the richest country in the world, and one of the most democratic, sprawling "Third World" slums and ghettos for large segments of the working class are part of the most modern cities. In that country, and others, many of the rich live in their own ghettos — fenced-off, privately-policed compounds, enclaves and fortresses of the money-lords, islands of the rich in the great social sea.

In such cities, and in the cities of less rich countries like Stalinist-capitalist China, vast numbers of people live in varieties of want. Great numbers in the cities are homeless. Many are cut off by poverty from modern medicine. In the most advanced society on earth, the USA, tens of millions of people exist without adequate medicine and medical care. Obamacare changed that, but not enough: it reduced the number without medical insurance from 18% to 11%. 33 million people!

B. But 7% more now have health insurance. You insist on seeing only the remaining 11%. Preconceived socialist nay-saying! Give them time.

A. For poor people who are sick, time is often what they haven't got, just as they haven't got money. And the prospects are not for continued improvement. In the USA, the percentage without health insurance is already rising again. Even in better-run countries like Britain, inequality is spiralling. Millions toil at insecure, ill-paid, draining jobs. They have little or no control over how their lives and energies are spent. Many rely on food banks and are ill-housed, while the billionaires lord it in ostentatious consumption and rule over our lives.

B. But the system works. It has allowed for improvement, and continues to allow for improvement.

A. The world economy collapsed into a great slump in 2007-8, and we are still not out of it a decade later. Around seven million workers, across the richer countries alone, lost their jobs and became unemployed. Real wages fell in Britain by 10%, and are not expected to get back to the 2008 level for another decade, unless the working-class movement acts to insist, as it well may. And Britain was by no means the hardest-hit country.

The bankers, everywhere, mad for profit, lent money, and borrowed money from each other, wildly and recklessly. They cared for nothing else except their revenues. Then they panicked when they realised that they were balancing on top of a gigantic pyramid of debts that would never be paid.

Millions upon millions of people fell victim to the relentless, reckless drive for private profit by the small minority which dominates economic and social life. The story of the banks here is not only about the banks, of course. It is the summing-up of the whole capitalist system, of which the banks are so central a part — its epitome.

B. Many "ordinary" people benefited from the credit splurge, you know. They were able to buy their homes because the banks were generous.

A. Yes, and an awful lot of them then found that their homes were owned by banks impatient for their loot. In America, the Promised Land of capitalism, six million households — six million! — had lost their homes by 2015 in an epidemic of bank foreclosures, because they couldn't meet the monthly mortgage-money repayments. What they had already paid was confiscated by the "generous" bank.

The bankers were driven to make reckless loans, to citizens and to each other, not by generosity but by greed. They went mad for money. Like the Gadarene swine in the bible story, possessed by the Devil, in their frenzy they stampeded over a cliff — pulling vast numbers of homeowners with them. They got madder and more reckless, the more money they made. Without the services which the banks provide, without the flow of money and credit, this society would seize up. It couldn't function. But the bankers run the banks as their private property, in their own interest.

It is astonishing, if you pause to think about it — the banks *are* their private property! An international class of billionaires, united in an attitude of patronising disdain towards the working class and other working people, ran and run the credit system which is essential to the whole of society for their own benefit, to make the maximum profit for themselves.

It would be hard to invent a better parable to illustrate what is wrong with capitalism than this true story, of which we are all part, and which pitched us into the worst economic and social slump for nearly a century. I put it to you that such a system is insane.

B. Insane? It's the most rational system in history.

A. Then god help humanity! The ways the governments responded in the emergency — the right-wing Bush administration in the USA as well as the New Labour neo-Thatcherite government in Britain — proves how nonsensical and crazy it all is. The governments had to take over and guarantee the functions of the banks — "temporarily". In Ireland, where we go to extremes, the Fianna Fail government took responsibility for *all* the banks' debts. Governments "nationalised" the losses of the banks, made "society" responsible for them.

B. What are you complaining about? Socialists think the government should intervene in the economy all the time.

A. Yes, but to serve the people. Here the governments served not only society but the same billionaires who had caused economic and social havoc.

B. The governments *had to* bail out the banks. The alternative was to let the whole system seize up, even to the extent that High Street cash-points would close.

A. Yes, because the great social engines of finance, on which everything in the society and economy depends, were the billionaires' private property, and run by them as engines of private enrichment. The necessary social role of the banks was tied to, merged with, and subordinated to, the exigencies of private ownership, and regulated by their drive for private gain. The banks were operated primarily to make profits for their private owners. And that brought society all across the world to a convulsive, juddering crisis. Then "society", via the governments, had to pay an immense ransom to rescue those whose greed had brought us all close to disaster.

B. To rescue society! The banks were too big to be allowed to fail.

A. Exactly! As someone aptly said: this is a system of privatised profit and socialised loss. That in a nutshell sums up what is wrong with capitalism as a whole. Of course, it's not only the banks.

Vast social complexes of production, exchange, communication, without which this society could not function, and on which the livelihoods of untold millions depend, are run as private property for the benefit of a comparatively small number of private owners. They are run in the interests of their owners no matter what it means for others or for society as a whole.

The official ideology stipulates worship of the market-as-god. The governments act as its high priests, enforcers, and protectors. Socialism, or even social action, is the devil's work.

Then we saw that the US and Britain were ruled by "social-istic" governments, selectively social-istic but social-istic all the same. We saw governments intervene drastically and substitute themselves for the operation of the markets. The right wing US government took over, or engineered the taking-over, of AIG, the biggest insurance company in the world, of most of the big banks, and of Fannie Mae and Freddie Mac, the two corporations that guaranteed around 90% of household mortgages in the USA. (And yet the newly "interventionist" US government did not "intervene" to stop six million foreclosures!) In Britain, the neo-Thatcherite Blair-Brown government took over several banks. The US administration of George W Bush and the Blair-Brown government of Britain assumed the social role which the failing banks had played, the role of financial organiser and regulator of the entire economy. They used the government power to channel many billions of dollars and pounds from tax-paying society to subsidise the banks.

B. The British prime minister, Gordon Brown, explained that if they had not intervened, if they had not played the role of organiser, financier, and guarantor of the financiers, then the high street cash-point machines would have closed down. "Society" would have seized up, as the US economy did when the banks closed their doors in the early 1930s. Or worse. That's why the governments did what they did.

A. Yes. It was an acknowledgement that uncontrolled markets and privately-owned banks had led us to the brink of social disaster. In the last resort, the all-ruling banks depended on social action by the overall representatives of society, the governments, to avert disaster, to cancel out the natural consequences for the bankers and for society of profiteer-led free markets.

B. It was judicious temporary government intervention. "Social-ism", if you like — but not your socialism!

A. No, not our socialism. If this "socialism", or "social-ism", or "society-ism", was undertaken in the interests of society, it was nonetheless bankers' social-ism, fat-cat social-ism. Bourgeois social-ism. In Marxist terms, state capitalism. It did, however, point to the fundamental rationale of Marxist socialism, the thing that makes it good sense and essentially invulnerable to the defeat, subversion or destruction of socialist parties, despite the often terrible human cost of those defeats: capitalism itself prepares and continually develops towards the socialist transformation of society. The government intervention in the crisis proved how important social action is, and how necessary — but this was socialism for the billionaires. Socialists want a socialism for all working people.

B. Oh, I agree that the bankers' vast bonuses should not be allowed.

A. "Everyone" agrees on that — and nobody can do anything very much about it. That neatly sums up our situation. Yes, the bonuses are obscene. But the bigger obscenity is the power we let these people and their system have over us, over society. The relationship summed up in the cliché idea of gunmen sticking up a bank is the opposite of the true relationship of the banks to society. The banks "stick up" the rest of society. Routinely. All the time. And, in 2007-8, spectacularly.

These institutions — let's stay with the example of the banks — operate like criminal gangs, like so many mafias, preying on the rest of society.

B. You exaggerate wildly. There's been big trouble since 2007-8, but in the long view that is just a blip. Mafias, indeed!

A. Do I exaggerate? The foreclosing US banks robbed six million households of the money they had paid on their mortgages, because they couldn't continue paying. Six million households: how many people is that? Take the US average household of 2.5 people, and that's 15 million. And surely some of the six million would already have paid back the loans, and were at that point paying only the interest on them. Mafias!

B. No. The banks operated within the law, the democratically made and controlled law.

A. That's the point! They operated like gangsters, but *gangsters who can make the laws*, with the government acting on their behalf.

B. You can't equate legal financial operations with illegal gangsterism.

A. Tell that to the six million families whose houses were confiscated! Of course there is a difference. But the similarities are telling. Woody Guthrie put it very well: "Some rob you with a six-gun, and some with a fountain pen".

Think about it another way. Billions of shares are bought and sold on the stock exchanges as a form of gambling. There are great financial cartels that organise the gamblers. In the real world, they are gambling with the livelihoods of those who work in enterprises which they use as gambling chips..

B. But it works.

A. Sometimes. In the 19th century people were outraged at stories of Russian aristocrats literally wagering their serfs in card games.

B. You want to make a comparison? You want to say these are identical things?

A. The clue to the difference is in the little word, serfs. These are not identical things. What strikes me, nonetheless, is how many points of comparison there are. The life prospects of a lot of workers, legally free workers, not serfs, are staked in these stock exchange gambles.

The 2013 strike by dockworkers in Hong Kong, one of the world's busiest ports, against Hutchison, the world's biggest container terminal operator, won wide support and made serious gains in wages.

The Social Morality of Capitalism

A. Look at it another way. In an era of wonderful, near-miraculous mass communications, tens and hundreds of millions live educationally in a world of ignorance, pseudo-knowledge, infinite credulity nourished on internet-legend and internet-scuttlebut. In intellectual, spiritual, and moral barbarism. Just glance at the programme lists on satellite TV. Much of it is on what used to be the level of kids' comics and the old film serials like Batman, Superman, and Captain Marvel. A mixture of science-fiction and tongue-in-cheek pseudo-mystical drivel. The most popular movies are of the same sort and on the same level. We see amazing technology in the service of profit-chasing commercial moronism and lowest-common-denominator social idiocy. We live in what someone satirically called an "idiocracy" run with small consideration in mind other than to make money for the already very rich. Commerce, and its market needs, modes, and conveniences — these are the givers of morality in our world, and its great universal role-model.

B. The markets give people what they want.

A. "The market" steers and educates people as to what they should want. The breakdown of old religious-based ethics and morality creates an urgent need for a rational, humanity-centred system of private and public morality, a morality based on human solidarity. The culture of commercial capitalism eats at the ties, linkages, and proper functioning of society. The prevailing morality, "the war of all against all", is the natural spirit, epitome, and morality of capitalism. This account-book morality is radically at odds with the needs of a humane and rational society. It sheds or demeans all other human considerations, everything other than the imperatives of trade, commerce, and money-making.

Capitalist market-modelled culture — consume as much as you can, always seek to do better than the next person — is irredeemably at odds with human solidarity. As Karl Marx and Frederick Engels put it in the Communist Manifesto: "the bourgeoisie has left remaining no other nexus between man and man than naked self-interest, than callous 'cash payment'."

B. You prefer the morality of the old religious mumbo-jumbo, laid down by the priests of a supposedly all-ruling but incredibly stupid God, obsessed with trivialities?

A. No. I choose a morality based on reason and human solidarity.

Everywhere in society now we have the twisted wrecks of old aspirations. In our world, solidarity is condemned and disdained at every turn. Inequality is all-pervasive, grotesque, and lauded.

For example, in Britain, the poor pay, proportionately, as much or more tax than the rich. Because of VAT, council tax, and other regressive taxes, a household in the bottom ten per cent pays 43% of its income in tax, while a household in the top ten per cent pays 35%.

The horrible paradox is that this is the same sort of class matrix as the privileges of the pre-1789 French nobility. Among the rich, the ethos of paying only what cannot be evaded is dominant. The tax workers' union PCS estimates the amount of tax evaded, avoided, or uncollected each year at £119 billion, about the same as the total NHS budget.

B. Maybe you have half a point. But your comparison with the pre-revolutionary French aristocracy is grotesque!

A. The reality is grotesque, not my comparison. Again, the private ownership of city land allows the charging of immense "taxes" on everybody who rents, or uses the services of those who rent. The Duke of Westminster and Earl Cadogan own much of central London and the Mosley family, the family of the old Fascist leader, Sir Oswald Mosley, much of central Manchester. This amounts to a system of robbery administered for the robbers by the state.

B. Ah — Henry George! Tax the landlords out of existence?

A. In itself not a bad idea. But we'll need a lot more than that to get rid of capitalism. There is now an attitude of Aztec-like fatalism towards capitalism, a superstitious helplessness in relation to the depredations of the market. Towards the capitalist priests tearing out human hearts to feed the great, greedy, all-powerful God, profit.

B. You can't equate ripping-out of hearts with high rents and tax evasion!

A. My comparison is of the fatalistic acceptance of horrors in both cases, even if different horrors. All horrors are not identical: yes, some are worse than others. But that does not justify or excuse the lesser horrors!

B. It is still preposterous.

A. The decline of old mainstream Christian churches gives place not to enlightenment and to something better, but to regression, to more dogmatic, more archaic, more primitive forms of religion, like Christian evangelism, and to an alarming extent to the spread of dogmatic political Islam in the West. To "wild" religion and to its sub-species like tarotry, "horoscopolatry", and a half-baked nature-worship, which is a stupefied form of rejection of modern society. Reason and knowledge, and respect for reason and knowledge, are at an immense disadvantage. In the USA, a politician cannot get elected unless he or she professes and practises a religion, or pretends to.

Baptists and other Christian sects from the most developed and most powerful country on earth export their reason-defying, emotion-driven, barbarous beliefs to Africa. One result of that is ultra-savage repression and legislation against homosexuality in Uganda and other African countries.

In the Muslim world, the immense oil-wealth of the rulers of such places as Saudi Arabia combines with the pressures, contradictions, and jarring interpenetrations of cultures to trigger volcanic eruptions of petrified, self-righteous, murderously militant jihadist superstition.

B. That's not capitalism! It's an irruption from the dark ages!

A. Yes, of course it is. But the Islamists are entwined with world capitalism. It's a malign example of what Marxists call "combined and uneven development".

B. Spare me the Marxist gobbledegook! So your main argument for socialism is a moral one? That's not what I understand to be the Marxist case.

A. No, my "main" argument is economic, social, and historical, and "moral" only in that context. But the state of public morality in our world is to my mind a summing-up of all that is wrong with capitalist society, its DNA, its spiritual aureole, its epitome. That is a central part of the historic indictment of capitalism made by Marx and other socialists. To the social and economic relations of capitalism, its public morality is the picture of Dorian Gray, the portrait that reveals the inner corruption, vicious, hideous, repressive, exploitative, worker-enslaving, even while the living face still looks healthy. Except that this portrait is not hidden away in an attic somewhere, like the painting in Oscar Wilde's fiction. You see it all around you. It hits you in the face. If you want to see what capitalism is, and what is wrong with it, look at the social and personal morality it has spawned and continually breeds.

B. Depravity, vice, horror is very much in the eye of the beholder, sometimes the neurotic beholder.

A. So is *refusal to see* your world. Ecological catastrophe looms, for lack of rational planning of economic and social development.

On such issues, the direct involvement of international corporations and their tame pre-paid scientists poisons public discourse. The big corporations spend vast sums through their advertising and public-relations agencies to lie and misrepresent things to serve their interests. The profit-fuelled corporations must go on driving for profit, even though their system now threatens ecological ruin, and their own ruination too. We are like ignorant, primitive farmers who do not know enough not to work the soil to an exhaustion which means destruction for themselves and their community — except that here the problem is not lack of knowledge, but the inability of knowledge, or considerations about the general interests of humankind, to control the profit-mongers, themselves caught in the terrible rush of profit-seeking, profit-mad capitalism. The profit drive here works to put out the social, ethical, historical, and forward-looking eyes of humankind.

To both capitalism and Stalinism, the people are essentially what farm beasts are to the farmer — creatures to be worked, exploited, and used up.

B. Farm animals are killed and eaten!

A. Ok — they don't actually consume the workers! They do everything short of that.

Socialism is the plain and obvious answer to the problems our world faces. By socialism, I mean the very opposite of Stalinism: rational, democratic planning of our social and economic affairs, which means also of our ecological affairs; the application of consistent reciprocal democracy (instead of war) to the solution of the economic, national, and religious conflicts of our world.

Socialism means consistent democracy on national questions, as well as on the political, , social, and economic fronts.

So, What Is Socialism?

B. Socialists are good at criticising and rubbishing the society we live in. You are less forthcoming about your own positive alternative to it.
A. The elaboration of a detailed picture of a future socialist society would be arbitrary and pointless, because we can't know in detail how things will evolve.
B. That puts people like me at a disadvantage. We defend what is, what we know, what critics also can see and know and denounce. You "defend" a vague and shadowy future, and say that in detail it is unknowable. What, positively, would a socialist society as you conceive of it be like?
A. Socialism is human solidarity, beginning as a system of working-class bonding in resistance to capitalist exploiters, and raised up, projected, to being the guiding principle of all society. It is the elimination of class exploitation by making the means of production, exchange, and communication collective social property, rather than, as now, private property run for private gain. It is the enthronement of unfettered reason armed with love, enlightenment, entrenched respect for individuals, and democracy in all the social, economic and political affairs of society. The socialists are the consistent democrats.
B. Love? Have I suddenly fallen down the rabbit-hole into a sloppy romance for pre-pubescent girls?
A. Love! Society will collectively own and democratically control and administer the bulk of productive wealth. Every major industry will be reorganised roughly like the National Health Service at its ideal best — with full provision for everyone's need as its governing principle. It will be democratically controlled by workers, by consumers, and by the overall community.

The privileges and perks of managers, officials, bureaucrats and shareholders will be abolished. There will be democratic self-rule in all aspects and on all levels of society and in the economy, in short, in all the circumstances and conditions of our lives — democratic self-rule that will be far more flexible, responsive and accountable than any government is today. Each electorate will control its representatives and be able to use a right of recall and re-election at any time. There will be a comprehensive living democracy in the social and economic affairs of humankind, where now at best there exists only pluto-democracy, money-dominated democracy

— shallow, often socially and economically impotent, mere-political democracy. The whole industrial structure can thus be planned, in broad outline, to meet human need.

That means no rich and no poor, no profit-as-goal and no wage-slavery. No private palaces and no homelessness. No jobless and no-one overworked on the treadmills of profit. The working week will be cut to a level which enables all to have ample free time to devote to social and political affairs and to self-development as individuals — by study, sport, art, handicrafts, friendship, travel, or whatever they wish that does not harm or hinder others. Socialism means liberty as well as economic planning. It includes economic planning by way of liberty, democracy, and enlightenment. To put it in well-known words, it is the realisation of liberty, equality, sorority, and fraternity.

B. That's still too vague and shadowy!

A. There is nothing vague or shadowy about it! Maybe the vagueness and shadowiness you perceive are an aspect of your wilful refusal to see this clearly.

B. Or maybe it's a result of built-in imprecision and vagueness in the ideas you expound. You know, on some levels — love as the cement of society, indeed! — what you say sounds almost religious to me.

A. Religion gathers into its maw many good human impulses, needs, and desires. As Karl Marx long ago noted: "Religion is the sigh of the oppressed, the heart of a heartless world". Religion turns life on its head, looking to supernatural agencies to intervene in this world. Socialism reclaims from religion the human desires which religion translates into mysticism, nonsense, prostration before imagined celestial beings.

Socialist ideas are built up from the history of capitalism, from working-class battles and other experiences, and from Marx's analysis of capital. Socialism will build on the science, the technology, the economic cooperation, the working-class solidarity, developed within capitalism, but free them from being poisoned by exploitation and all that goes with it. Stop them from being thwarted by the profit-drive. The economy will be run in a cooperative way, for the benefit of society, and not for private profit. Operated in the interests not of profit for a few, but of everyone.

Positively, at the most basic level, I see socialism as a world run like a good, caring, prosperous, egalitarian family is run now: sharing, taking care of everyone's needs, treating all the children of the society equally, educating everyone, fully and properly. A world run according to human solidarity, without racism, sexism, or built-in disadvantage or privilege for anyone or for any groups or classes of people.

Socialism would end the compulsion upon which capitalist society rests, for the workers to sell their labour power — their active lives, most of their active hours of life — to people intent on making money out of their labour power, that is, on exploiting them. Now employers put them to work, on the employer's terms, for hours each day during which the workers create for the employer much more than the value of the wage the employer pays. The bedrock class struggle — the workers' struggle for higher wages and shorter hours, and the bosses' resistance to that — is a tussle over possession of the wealth which workers create over and above their wages and which then becomes, automatically, the property of the buyer of labour power.

B. What you call working-class solidarity is narrow, obtuse ganging-up on someone else, the people you call the plutocrats. And, often, on other workers.

A. Working-class solidarity here and now is a weapon in the class war: workers stand together and look out for each other. It is also a manifestation inside capitalism of the human solidarity of the socialist society we will build, without disadvantaging any subsection of humankind, as women and people of colour are disadvantaged now, even after the progress made towards gender and race equality in the 20th century. Working-class solidarity embodies here and now the common humanity of human beings living in the dog-eat-dog conditions of capitalism. As I've said, socialism will be a world run according to what William Morris called "fellowship".

B. That daft medievalist!

A. He was a Marxist!

B. That daft Marxist, then.

A. You know, much of your slant on society and on socialism depends on sheer dumb prejudice and shell-backed ignorance. The socialist world would be governed by the idea of unlimited and unstinting human solidarity and fellowship, whereas in capitalist society, the dominant ethos is that each person seeks ways to rob the neighbours, to steal an advantage, to monopolise possession of a desirable job. It is what Frederick Engels and earlier socialists described as the war of all against all.

B. It is human life as it is and as it has to be. It is human nature embodied and expressed in social relations and social arrangements. It is the natural state of human affairs.

A. It is only the natural state of capitalist affairs.

B. In any case, as somebody probably said, the strongest argument against socialism is the socialists themselves! Misfits and oddballs!

A. Socialists are people who by political instinct and conviction side with the oppressed and exploited, victims of malign power and of cruel indifference. We fight racism. We fight for women's equality with men, and against all the privileged of capitalist society. The left in history has been a tremendous force for progress, enlightenment, liberty, tolerance, and freedom. It has fought tyrannies and tyrants, and the rule of priests and prelates. It has fought for civil rights and civil liberties, for free speech and free thought, and against censorship. It has organised and shaped labour movements that have established and broadened working-class rights against employers and their states. We have fought fascism, Stalinism, plutocracy, capitalism. The real left, in any situation, are the consistent democrats.

We now look back and wonder at old tolerance for old evil, cruelty and stupidity. Others, living in the better world socialists will win, will look back at us and ask: how did they tolerate a world in which millions of children die each year from avoidable diseases and malnutrition.

Socialists who spend their lives fighting these and other present-day obscenities are frequently depicted as odd, neurotic people who should "get a life". A more enlightened age will think it was the people who kept their heads down, remaining "quiet", "private", narrow-focused in the face of social obscenities, who were the odd ones. People like you!

B. Your ideas are fond and blatant ideologising. That is why socialism is unpopular now. People have seen through it.

A. Well, yes, of course. Marx and Engels put it well: the ruling ideas in every society are the ideas of the ruling class. The class struggle also takes place on the level of ideas and conceptions of class and of society.

B. And the fact that so many of us see it differently settles your hash!

A. Events such as the 2007-8 economic semi-collapse of capitalism speak powerfully for our picture of reality, the Marxist picture.

B. But they say nothing positively in favour of your view of socialism.

A. Socialism is rooted in capitalism. Marx put it well: it will "set free the elements of the new society with which old collapsing bourgeois society itself is pregnant".

Socialism Is Discredited By Stalinism?

B. But why on earth should I be a socialist? Socialism is the bogeyman my mother threatened me with — except that socialism was real. Why should anyone in the 21st century be a socialist? What socialism? There is no viable, clean, uncontaminated socialism left. Jumping out of the capitalist frying pan into the Stalinist fire, or risking that we will end up again in totalitarian Stalinism, makes no sense. Learn from history! Socialists today are people incapable of learning from history — fond and fixated sentimentalists, fantasists, masochists, and, all of you, political fuckwits. The much-cited quotation puts it neatly: those who do not learn from history are likely to repeat it. That's you, mate, and the count-them-on-one-hand little tribe of your co-thinkers.

A. Yes, socialism is much less of a political force now than it once was. Trotsky called Stalinism the "syphilis" or, again, the "leprosy" of the labour movement. It undermined, sapped, butchered, and discredited the old socialist movement. It turned the Stalinist-controlled part of the labour movement into an enemy of liberty, equality, fraternity, and unfettered reason — in short, into an enemy of socialism as it was before Stalin and as it was held to against Stalin by socialists and Bolshevik anti-Stalinist diehards, in the first place Trotsky. Today the socialists do their political work amidst ideological ruins and the poisonous ideological vapours that constitute the legacy of Stalinism. Old socialism, pre-Stalinist and anti-Stalinist socialism, is still half-buried beneath the ruins of the collapsed Stalinist system. But it exists!

B. All through history there have been people like you — recklessly putting at risk what has been achieved, that which is, in pursuit of untried and allegedly better alternatives — the benefits that supposedly might come into being in the future. That some innovations have worked out well does not prove that all innovations do, or have done! In fact, the experience is that they don't. Look at socialism in practice, in the old USSR, or in China!

A. It was not socialism; it was Stalinism, the rule of a privileged, exploitative ruling class over the people. Right now, in your head, socialism is mainly a shadowy, and thereby all the more terrifying, bogeyman.

B. Ah yes, nobody understands it but you. And Stalinism had nothing to do with socialism!

A. Marxists base their socialism on certain social and economic achievements of capitalism — in the first place the development of the productive forces to a very high level, a level capable of producing the basic needs of life in abundance for everyone. The Stalinist system came to power by overthrowing working-class rule in Russia. According to Marx and according to those who led the Russian Revolution, the basic social and economic prerequisites of their socialism were not present in Russia. The workers could take power there, and did. To go on to build socialism, they needed the partnership of the advanced countries like Germany, France, and Britain. By the criteria of Marx and of the Bolsheviks, Russia alone could not build socialism. The Stalinists proclaimed themselves to be building socialism in one country, although backward Russia was way behind the advanced capitalist countries.

So what is wrong about refusing to accept Stalinism as "socialism" in the Marxist sense? The perversity here is yours. You are in the grip of the post-Stalinist jitters and political-philosophical funk. Get over Stalinism! Look around you at the foulness that immerses us all under capitalism, and the squandering of the opportunities that capitalism's development of the productive forces gives us for creating a better social world.

B. You ignore history: you juggle frivolously and irresponsibly with abstract theory, fond ideals, early socialist utopian blueprints! It's irrelevant. Stalin was the real socialist. Stalinism was the real socialism, the practical consequence of a socialist coup in 1917. Stalin and his team were the people who made socialism work — for a while. You want to slough off the responsibility that goes with acknowledging that Stalinism was the very essence of socialism. The only possible socialism.

A. Large numbers of people of my political persuasion "sloughed off" Stalinism when it was at its acme. They lived in its Gulag or died fighting it outside Russia — in Spain, Greece, France, Vietnam, and other places — in the name of socialism, of working-class communism, of the October 1917 revolution, of Bolshevism, and of social and political democracy.

I'm telling you what socialism meant before Stalinism, and to the Marxist critics and enemies of Stalinism, in the first place, to Trotsky and his comrades. The history of Stalinism was simultaneously the history of socialist anti-Stalinism. Stalinism has not been the only self-proclaimed socialism. Authentic working-class socialists measured the USSR and the fate of the working class under Stalinism against socialist hopes, perspectives, norms, basic Marxist theory. They measured it against the programme in the name of which the Russian Revolution was made; against the socialist commitment to working-class freedom and democracy. They advocated a working-class revolution against Stalinist autocracy. Those critics included the leaders of the Russian Revolution, which you say evolved smoothly, naturally, and organically into Stalinism! In the mid 1920s most of the surviving Bolsheviks came out against Stalinism at one point or another — that is, against the bureaucratic dictatorship taking shape. Lenin did, denouncing Stalin from his deathbed. Trotsky did, in 1923. Zinoviev did, Kamenev did. From late 1927 Stalin drove the Bolshevik opposition into internal exile in Russian wilderness places, then into labour camps. Then Stalin massacred most of the surviving 1917 revolutionaries, leaders and rank-and-file members alike.

Stalin massacred even those who in the disputes of the 1920s had made up the Stalin faction. Of the 1,996 party delegates at the 100%-Stalinist "Congress of Victors" in 1934, Stalin's gang had 1,108 arrested, and maybe 700 killed, within three years. Of the 139 members elected to the "Central Committee" at that Congress, Stalin would kill 98. And yet you insist that Bolshevism and Stalinism, the murdered and their murderers, are identical!

B. We refuse to let Trotsky in his anti-Stalinist phase get socialism off the hook.

A. Yes. You are shameless ideological profiteers on Stalinism. You take over and use for your own purposes the big Stalinist lie that Stalinism was socialism; Bolshevism; Marxism come to life. This is the United Front of the Liars Against Socialism!

B. No, it's the United Front of the Truth-Tellers Against Lies and Against Socialism! Anyone who knows modern history will tell you, Stalinism was socialism. The Stalinists told the truth about socialism and their relation to it. They gave their system its true name: socialism.

A. You are ridiculously unscrupulous! You retail the old lies of old Stalinism on behalf of the other, the bourgeois, enemy of socialism. You follow in the tracks of the leaders of the Stalinist counter-revolution in the USSR in the 1920s and 30s. They wrote and rewrote history, threading and weaving a mass of totalitarian lies into its fabric. You endorse and spread their great lie, that they represented socialism, Bolshevism, the working class in power, continuity with the 1917 revolution.

The anti-Stalinist socialists like Trotsky showed, by their words and deeds and by their fate, that Stalinism had nothing in common with the aims, the modes, the methods, and the objectives of real communism and socialism; that communism and Stalinism were, as Trotsky put it, like Cain and Abel (the two brothers in the bible Book of Genesis, one of whom murdered the other).

The choice is: either to measure Stalinism against socialist politics and socialist theory before Stalinism and thus put Stalinism in its proper historical perspective. Or arbitrarily set up Stalinism as socialism, and as the only possible socialism. That is shoddy polemic, not serious discussion. You rest entirely on the fact that Stalin said it was socialism, and said, no less falsely, that it was rooted in the October Revolution. The Stalinists slaughtered the Bolshevik party. The Stalinists killed more socialists than Hitler and Mussolini and Franco combined! You use Stalinism to rule out, wipe out, crush all serious discussion of socialism and of the real history of the Russian workers' revolution and its ultimate fate. Of the Stalinist counter-revolution that destroyed it. It could be said that here you use the historical fact of Stalinism in a totalitarian way — indeed, in a Stalinist way!

You bury yourself in the crassest know-nothing anti-socialist claptrap, using Stalinism as your excuse! You avoid discussing socialism beyond making that false identification of Stalinism with socialism. And you thereby suppress rational discussion of a viable alternative to capitalism.

B. Facts are facts! Every thoroughgoing attempt to make socialism has resulted in tyranny. Maybe the intentions of the socialists were good. But the results were horrific. Every time. It's a truly terrible story, the story of 20th century socialism...

A. Of 20th century Stalinism!

B. ... And yet you still advocate "socialism"! Socialism? It's not a lie that Stalinism was socialism, or that socialism was Stalinism. It is the plain truth. For you and yours, it is the unsuppressable damning truth. You are stuck to it like a bird trapped in sticky bird-lime. Flapping your ideological wings won't save you.

A. It is you and yours who are stuck and limed in the Stalinist lies. They disable you. They make you politically stupid. They cut you off from the only rational answer to the urgent needs of society for economic and political democracy, for rational planning of the economy, and for responsible ecology. Real socialism is the precondition of continued human progress, and, maybe, for the survival of civilisation itself.

You claim that the rulers of the totalitarian Stalinist states naming themselves as socialists entitles you to identify socialism with Stalinism and to say that Stalinism was the end of the road for honest socialist aspirations.

B. And your denial of it is pitiable.

A. OK. What's sauce for the goose is sauce for the gander, as they say.

SOCIALISM IS DISCREDITED BY STALINISM?

The rulers of the Stalinist states didn't only call themselves communists and socialists; they called themselves democrats too, and their system democratic. The official name of the satellite states — Poland, Czechoslovakia, Hungary, etc. — was "People's Democracies". Their international magazine in the 1940s and 50s was, believe it or not, called: *For a Lasting Peace, for a People's Democracy*. Stalin proclaimed the advent of "full democracy" in the new Stalinist constitution of 1936. It was "the most democratic Constitution in the world", its admirers said, and they were not all dyed-in-the-lies Stalinists. They included the venerable British Fabians, Beatrice and Sidney Webb, and many other "non-Stalinist" Stalinists

If the Stalinists' fraudulent claim to be socialists damns and stigmatises all socialists for ever after, and Stalinism's collapse proves socialism impossible — why does their no less fraudulent claim to be democrats not discredit democracy?

B. Because real democracies — what you call bourgeois, plutocratic democracies — existed side-by-side with the Stalinist "democracies", and continue to exist and multiply long after the collapse of European Stalinism. Show me an example of working class socialism side-by-side with what you call the fraudulent socialism of the Stalinists! Then I might accept the point you're trying to make.

A. No socialist state or society existed alongside Stalinism. But there were socialists and socialist movements that existed side-by-side with it and fought against Stalinism in the name of the socialist ideas which existed before Stalinism. The anti-Stalin socialists counterposed that socialism to Stalinism, and based a radical critique of Stalinism on it.

The Marxist case for socialism is that humanity must go forward to something new, something better than the capitalist or Stalinist present or past. That can only be socialism, the socialism of the socialists before Stalinism and of those who fought against Stalinism. The Stalinist states had nothing to do with democracy of any kind. But they had nothing to do with socialism, either.

Think about the fact that masses and masses of people believed in the "democracy" proclaimed by the Stalinists (just as many people believe that the truncated and severely limited democracy we have in countries like Britain is the best democracy possible). The Stalinist ideologists argued, when they deigned to argue, and convincingly to a lot of people, that things like housing, assured employment, public health care, etc., were the real stuff of democracy in the USSR. Conflating distinct things, they redefined democracy as no unemployment and things like that.

B. The virtues they claimed for the USSR — housing, for example — were not really there either, any more than democracy was.

A. Indeed! But you in turn say about bourgeois democracy that the mere trappings of democracy are the real and full democracy, irrespective of the social and economic reach of the democracy, or the lack of it. That's not exactly what the Stalinists did, but it's in the same family of misrepresentation by way of substituting something else for what should be discussed. In your case, substituting bourgeois-democratic trappings for real, multi-dimensional collective self-rule.

B. On democracy those socialist...

A. Stalinist!

B. ... arguments ducked the issue. They were sleights of mind. They substituted something else for the thing under debate — democracy, self-rule by the demos, the people. People politically enslaved may have all the social amenities you like, though of course they didn't, and in a society of scarcity couldn't; but they don't have democracy.

A. Again, yes indeed. We can agree on that. But mark you this: a major reason why people thought Stalinism democratic was the social shallowness of bourgeois democracy — how little real control over society it gives us. That's what made them receptive to the Stalinist demagogues who substituted lying patter about jobs and housing, etc., for considerations of political and socialist democracy.

B. Socialism is the eternal virgin in its own head but — excuse my old-fashioned, politically-incorrect language — a scabby whore in reality. Good works, not good intentions! Socialism? All fine words and intentions, and, once in power, something else entirely. Give it up! You're not fooling anyone any more. The idea that socialism can revive, or even survive as a set of ideas among sensible people is preposterous. It is a bit like the Trinity (three persons in one god), or the Real Presence (the little bit of communion bread is literally, not symbolically, the body and blood of Christ). You will get believers still, but not among seriously rational people.

To believe in the revival of socialism, you need to have a very low opinion of people's intelligence. You can fool some of the people all of the time, and all the people some of the time, but not with "socialism", any more, thank God! People learn, albeit painfully. And they don't forget. They remember.

A. Yes! People learn, and will go on learning. And nothing is more obvious now, in the still unresolved world capitalist crisis that opened in 2007-8, than that capitalism, which was the dominant system even in the 20th century world that included Stalinism (Stalinism, not socialism!), has self-destructive contradictions which it cannot quell or resolve.

B. Capitalism has contradictions? Yes — but it is not dead. The capitalists learn. You refuse to learn.

A. The capitalists supposedly learned from the great slump after the stock-market crash of 1929. Governments imposed restrictions on bankers and devised new state-spending and credit policies designed to avoid similar things in the future. Has it worked? It hasn't!

B. It worked for a long time. Like democracy, capitalism may be riddled with faults — but all the alternatives are worse. That is what history tells us. You refuse to listen.

A. Listen to yourself! Your argument is essentially that because some people calling themselves socialists and communists acted in ways that contradicted all the promise of something better than capitalism which old socialism seemed to offer; because they created Stalinism — something worse than capitalism — therefore socialism is and deserves to be discredited. The implicit assertion is that capitalism is thereby rendered acceptable and that the socialist critique of capitalism can be brushed aside. No it can't! Why? Because we live still in the grip of a crazily rapacious and anti-human capitalism. Capitalism generates anti-capitalist socialism!

B. I think most people would say my conclusion about socialism is common sense. Your "socialism" is a picture of the Virgin Mary on the walls of a brothel — or of Gandhi or Tolstoy on the walls of a homicide chamber! The pictures would not affect what went on in those places — and only fools would define the places by the pictures on the wall.

A. It's either-or. Did socialism and Marxism exist before Stalinism? Yes, they did. Did socialists counterpose socialism to the Stalinist counterfeit? Yes they did. Therefore socialism cannot justly be defined by Stalinism. Stalinism must be measured and judged by the earlier socialist goals, norms, and aspirations, and by the yardsticks of Stalin's Marxist and Bolshevik opponents. And of their fight to the death against it. Rosa Luxemburg justly said that the Bolsheviks in 1917 saved the honour of international socialism. The Bolsheviks who died fighting Stalinism — most of the surviving Bolsheviks from 1917, with Trotsky at their head — saved the honour of Bolshevik international socialism. They saved and sustained and passed on authentic socialism.

Clockwise from top left: Leon Trotsky, who led both the 1917 uprising and the Bolshevik rearguard resistance to Stalinism; Natalia Sedova, Trotsky's companion, who continued the fight into the 1950s; and Rosa Luxemburg, killed by a right-wing gang operating under the aegis of the Social Democrats in Germany in 1919.

Part 2: Socialism and human nature

Human nature

B. Your socialist project flies in the face of the natural laws of society and of human nature! Capitalism is an expression of humankind's deepest impulses, harnessed to produce good effects by the market, the wonders-working market. You can't suppress or supersede that.

A. I know! Human beings are just wild animals, underneath? The naked ape?

B. Exactly. Nature itself is the opposite of your benign, or would-be benign, utopia-mongering and your sloppy sentimentalising over humankind. You can't change human nature! Humanity remains animal. Human nature — competitive, individualist, selfish, predatory — produces, protects, and preserves capitalism.

A. And the other way round. Capitalism evokes, encourages, rewards certain human traits — greed, oppression, etc. — what you think of as full human nature.

B. Predominant aspects of human nature.

A. If that were true, then why did we not have capitalism all back through history? We have had slave societies, feudal societies, "oriental-despotic" societies (ancient India and China, Inca Peru). The idea that capitalism is eternal is simply ignorant, or, for some, wish-thinking.

B. Don't be a smart-arse. You know what I mean: human beings are animals which prey on other animals. It's our deepest nature. And it correlates with capitalism and its ways.

A. Society remoulds our animal natures and impulses to an enormous extent. You may be broke or hungry and have an impulse to rob someone or break a shop window to get what you want, but the great bulk of civilised humanity will not act on such impulses.

B. What about the riots in 2011 in London, when people looted electronic goods stores?

A. The rarity of things like that reinforces my point.

B. They are rare because of the fear that the likelihood of state reprisals instills in people. Fear rules, not social feeling or innate altruism.

A. It is not just fear. That may inhibit some people. Mostly it is the sense of right and wrong, the awareness that society could not run if many people behaved that way. A desire to keep faith with others in society.

B. And your point?

A. As a rule, human beings are self-aware, self-controlling, self-shaping, self-reshaping. Natural animalist impulses are, for most people, most of the time, educated into submission to the higher order we in society have made for ourselves and of ourselves. We can aspire to a society governed by something higher than the dog-eat-dog morality which capitalism teaches and which you accept and glorify.

There is nothing in that aspiration which requires us to idealise human nature. Marx once said of himself that he identified with what an ancient Greco-Roman, Terence, said: Nothing human is alien to me.

B. Not everything he said or quoted is rubbish, then!

A. You could adapt that idea to: "Nothing animal is alien to humankind". At the start we are animals, and then animals who have developed themselves and gained consciousness of themselves — human beings. And not to libel our cousins, the animals, the fact is that much animal behaviour is altruistic. It is only human beings that prey systematically on their own kind.

To cite only one of the many, sometimes surprising, examples which the old anarchist Kropotkin collected in a whole book on the subject: "I was struck with the extent of mutual assistance which [crabs] are capable of bestowing upon a comrade in case of need. One of them had fallen upon its back in a corner of the tank, and its heavy saucepan-like carapace prevented it from returning to its natural position. Its comrades came to the rescue, and for [hours] they endeavoured to help".

B. Socialist solidarity for crabs! Now you are turning into a disciple of dear old St Francis, who preached to his brothers, the birds and the seals!

A. That is, indeed, a strange and unexpected example. That is why I cite it. Kropotkin was a natural scientist by profession, and there he told of what he had seen. Even if you think Kropotkin saw in the crabs what he wanted to see, the fact remains. The process of evolution from ape to human, from humanoid hunter-gatherer to our present tremendous ability to manipulate and in some respects control inanimate nature, is a long process of self-construction and self-reconstruction, in which we have made and then again re-made ourselves. That is basic: humankind makes and remakes itself. Nurture refracts nature, shapes and determines its social manifestations. It does that now. It can do it differently.

B. The aspiration to the socialist world you want, a world governed by fellow-feeling and human solidarity...

A. William Morris's consistent universal "fellowship"...

B. ... is hopeless. That aspiration, too, in you is old Christianity disguised: "All things bright and beautiful... The good God made them all". No, he didn't! Man made — invented — God. There is darkness, as well as light, and rather more of it. Learn from history! Accept the reality! Go with the grain! Not only the Stalinists, but the Nazis too, were what they were because they tried to reshape society according to an impossible, crazy ideal. *Leave well enough alone!*

A. Some wise old ape probably grunted that idea at another one who swung down from the trees and tried to walk upright. Your ancestor, one of the mates of the woman who invented agriculture, probably beat her for wasting good eating-seed by putting it in little holes she made in the ground.

B. And the ape just down from the trees probably replied: We apes can do anything. As soon as I learn to walk, I'll climb to the top of the tree, flap my wings, and fly like the eagle. So, I haven't got wings? I'll learn to grow a pair after I have learned to walk!

A. And yet the far distant descendants of that ape did learn to fly! Not by growing wings, it is true, but we fly nonetheless. The development of humankind's mastery of nature showed that growing wings, or adding bird-like wings to a mechanical structure, as Michelangelo tried to do, was not the way. There were other ways, and we discovered them. What your brave old ape wanted was realised, though not as she or he had imagined it could be.

As Trotsky put it: "The material premise of communism should be so high a development of the economic powers of man that productive labour, having ceased to be a burden, will not require any goad, and the distribution of life's goods, existing in continual abundance, will not demand — as it does not now in any well-off family or 'decent' boarding-house — any control except that of education, habit and social opinion. Speaking frankly, I think it would be pretty dull-witted to consider such a really modest perspective 'utopian'."

B. Said the man who slaughtered his enemies in the Russian civil war!

A. Enemies who slaughtered his comrades and who amidst other horrors perpetrated the worst anti-Jewish pogroms known to history before Hitler. All your arguments that socialism is "against human nature" are proven false by history. It is true that basic human drives — hunger for survival, food, sex, putting self and family first — are instinctive and can't disappear. But Trotsky was right. People can be educated, and are educated and re-educated all the time. It is plain fact that prevailing conceptions of what is right or wrong, acceptable or unacceptable, have changed and changed again as society has changed. From age to age, the way that basic instinctual drives are harnessed, refracted, redirected, expressed in relations with other human beings, has changed. Brutus, Shakespeare's "noblest Roman of them all", thought it morally right that people who owed him money should be imprisoned: that is, deprived of freedom and the chance to earn a living, in some cases condemned to starve to death. We know better. We have learned better.

B. Have we? And have we learned the right lessons? Much of what you call the class struggle in history has been the struggles between debtors and creditors, all the way back to ancient society. It is right that debtors should be penalised, and they are. One of the great bold statements of social law and the healthy society was made by an Irish government minister in the 1920s, Kevin O'Higgins, when he defined civilisation as a society in which the bailiff was able to function without fear of being shot.

A. The good part of that story is that he himself was shot dead on his way to Mass one Sunday morning in 1927.

B. You approve?

A. He had worked hard during the civil war of 1922-3 and after to earn what, finally, he got. It couldn't have happened to a better candidate for it.

B. That means you approve.

A. I don't weep. Take chattel slavery. In the ancient world, and long after, nobody, not the philosophers, nor the early Christians, saw moral wrong in slavery, or in setting gladiator slaves to fight and kill each other to provide spectators with sport. It's a myth that the Christians once in power stopped the gladiator-killing shows. There is some hidden chattel slavery in Britain now, and a lot of it in the wider world, but society condemns it and punishes those who inflict it on other people.

Once we thought it right that kings should have absolute power of life and death and social regulation.

Not long ago in historical time it was thought right, and found to be morally acceptable, that children, even very small children, should go to work in dangerous factories or be made to crawl up sooty chimneys. When Parliament first regulated child labour, it cut the hours, but it was suggested that, instead, the morally upright Victorian capitalists should work double shifts of children on the shorter hours.

B. All those things have been rectified.

A. That's the point. They were once thought necessary and therefore good and moral. Many aspects of capitalism which you defend and think normal will in future society be condemned as we condemn now notorious old abuses.

B. Dream on! In fact, you prove only that the reform of abuses happens when enough people think it necessary.

A. I'm showing that moralities change. Pioneers began the work of changing the previous validation of existing social horrors. A large part of European and American society used to think it right to discriminate against Jews and persecute them; some, that it was a moral duty to persecute or murder them. For centuries, it was all right to enslave black people to forced labour. For a long time, it was all right in the USA to work them to death.

Not so long ago a woman's citizenship was subsumed into that of her husband. Legally, children had only one parent, the father; a woman's property became her husband's. What kind of "crank", what degree of crankiness, would it take now to advocate any of those things that were once prevalent? Or defend them? Take a case that shouldn't be forgotten, but is. At the end of the 19th century, a young couple, members of the Marxist Social Democratic Federation, announced that, not believing in marriage, they were going to live together without the blessing of priest or the licence of magistrate. The parents of the woman, Edith Lanchester, committed her to an asylum for the insane. The couple were eventually forced into a legal marriage. By the way, the daughter of that couple became a well-known actress, Elsa Lanchester.

B. Ah, the "Bride of Frankenstein" herself. That figures. Bet she was a socialist. Frankenstein too, of course. And the monster as well, maybe?

A. Less than a hundred years ago in Britain, women did not have the Parliamentary vote, and neither did vast numbers of men who lacked the property qualifications. Or take sexuality. The sexual freedom we have now is only about half a century old. Our sexual morality today would seem foul and degenerate according to people in the malign grip of the recent old sexual morality. We live now in what used to be Sodom and Gomorrah! Not so long ago, tremendous restraints were placed on the expression of this basic human drive. Christian morality and social stigma imposed a senseless, murdering set of restraints on our sexuality. People who believed that God made us, also believed that godly morality demanded that human beings fight to suppress the nature which they believe their god had given them. What changed? Essentially, there were changes in the technology and the possibilities of birth control — "the pill" — sexuality was uncoupled from procreation, and soon uncoupled from the old morality. Sexual liberation, a sex-morality revolution, followed. Today in Britain many people coming from Islamic societies look on typical women who follow the prevailing sex-morality as being in effect prostitutes. Some Christians, too, are outraged, though in Britain they no longer count for all that much. There is a clash of two moralities: the new and the old. Savage old sexual morality comes into conflict with the new. The demystification of sex in the last half-century is a tremendous step forward, though we have quite a way to go.

B. Moralities change. Human nature doesn't.

A. Morality and legality "regulate" the expression of "human nature". People in the future will look at our capitalist society, in which, in order to live, people have to hire out to private individuals and companies intent on making profit out of their labour and to do their will for so many hours a week, as a variant of slavery, as "wage-slavery", as Marx put it. They will see the private ownership by people like Rupert Murdoch of newspapers and TV stations as we now see a world in which prelates laid down the law on what people could think. They will see it as absurd and radically incompatible with proper democracy. A lot less than half a century ago, it was considered right, moral, and necessary in Britain that school children should be beaten, frequently, regularly, by their teachers, and, at whim, by their parents and other "guardians". A lot of bullying and violence by parents against children still goes on, and legally parents have the right to beat children and to treat them in a way that they would be prosecuted for with another adult; but the old violence isn't considered "right" any more. "Human nature" is channelled to new expressions as society evolves, as we become more enlightened.

B. Not necessarily for the better! In any case, you mis-state things. Human nature is not as easy to modify and control as you wish-think it is.

A. But it can be modified in its expression and its social manifestations. It has been modified, is being modified. The history of social behaviour and social morality, of shifting ideas of right and wrong, proves what I say to be true. What would be the opposite of wish-thinking — wish-armoured refusal-to-think? Wish-denial? That's what you are doing here.

B. Again, you juggle irresponsibly with words — mere words! — and ideals. Reality is much harsher and more intractable than you think. Stubborn human individualism is the unsurpassable barrier to socialism.

A. Then let me tell you the strongest reason why the idea that capitalism corresponds to human nature is nonsense. In the oldest human societies we know about, long before capitalism, long before any class-stratified society, the sense of belonging to the collective is stronger than the sense of individual self. It was like that for god-knows how many hundreds of human generations. Individualism is itself a product of social and human development. In turn it is modified by further human development.

B. So now your socialist ideal takes as its model primitive groups of hunter-gatherers wandering in the primeval forests. We will go from primitive communism to… primitive communism!

A. This time, not primitive. This time, in a society which can exercise a tremendous degree of control over natural and social environments. In terms of the argument about human nature and capitalism and socialism, don't the facts about the earliest human societies say something to you?

B. Yes, thank god for rugged individualism!

A. Moving on from primitive collectivism and to the development of individualism was progress. But our instinctual "human nature" was not different in "primitive communism" from what it is now.

B. So it's back to the old Stone Age! That's your idea of human progress? That's your socialism for the 21st century?

A. Forward to a world in which the sense of human interconnectedness, solidarity, and fellowship is revived on a higher level of human ability to produce and reproduce the material means of life.

B. And individualism? You concede that was progressive in its time.

A. Individualism and a strong and governing sense of belonging to a great social interdependence are not in contradiction: they are complementary.

B. You are feeding me paradox-dialectics again! Gobbledegook!

A. You know what the great paradox here is? Individuation that produces individualism, the development of diverse minds and personalities, is very limited under capitalism: that is one of the things socialists criticise in capitalist society. It is one of the many great possibilities opened up before humankind by capitalism that capitalism can not and does not deliver for most of its citizens. Under wage-slavery, most people are compelled to spend most of their energy being "cogs in the machine" of production-for-profit. At best they can hope to develop their individualism in a very limited way outside work hours. And there they are seized on by commercialised capitalist culture. The "mass media" work against individual, critical, creative, innovative thinking, outside the conventional wisdom.

B. Often they work against serious thinking of any sort, creative or beaten-track-following!

A. Indeed. We live in the sugar-and-sex nexus of a commercial civilisation. Sugar in as many products as possible, sex used at varying conscious and subliminal levels to sell everything. Tremendous technologies of education, enlightenment, democratic participation, churn out Rupert Murdoch's news, commerce-ridden and commerce-corrupted spectator sport, brutish and misogynist pornography, TV programs like Jerry Springer's and others, exploiting ignorant, semi-literate victims of our educational system and of capitalism in general — sometimes it is the equivalent of the once-popular sports of bear-baiting and lunatic-tormenting. Everything is corrupted, tainted, and debased. Politics is reported as a branch of spectator sport or show business, a variant of fantasy football. Politicians are discussed for their "performance", and never mind the substance of what they are saying, or "should" say. People need to see themselves in elective, notional, tribes of football clubs, rock star fanship, networkings, etc.

In terms of work and training for work, people are stereotyped mass products. A once very common expression amongst socialists, which I've come to dislike thoroughly, "the masses" sums that up. In a world of material well-being, of democratic collectivism, individualism would flower in a way it can never flower under capitalism.

B. So you say! In fact the herd mentality too is part of human nature. Not a good part, either, I agree. On one level, your socialism is an appeal to that herd mentality.

A. I've shown you that operational or predominant human nature is not something static and fixed. That human nature includes many traits and possibilities. Remember that people in certain societies and with a certain conditioning are even capable of eating, cannibalising, other people.

B. Tosh! We have gone so far beyond that.

A. Yes, of course we have. Sort of! But isn't exploiting people as wage labour a form of "cannibalising" them, or close to that? What else is it to take someone's active life, their time, their qualities, their potential, and to use them to make money for yourself? You thereby consume a life, even if the idea of eating the flesh of those you "consume" revolts you.

B. That's just a fanciful identification of vastly different things.

A. I do not say that they are exactly the same thing. What I'm insisting upon is that human nature is socially malleable. It has, and has had, all sorts of possibilities. The question is what propensities a given society, or a given state, or a given class, encourages to develop, and what it discourages. Capitalist commercialism and its morality stifles some of the best, most human, and most humane potentialities. Capitalist society prizes, rewards, and glorifies those who prey on other people.

That is not, or not just, human nature. That is also nurture — what capitalist society makes of a human nature that also has vastly different possibilities, which capitalism tends to treat with contempt, inhibit, stifle, and eliminate.

B. Scratch a red, and you find a soft and stupid sentimentalist, oozing fond wet nonsense about humankind. An idiot who thinks that Christ's Sermon on the Mount and Kant's categorical imperative can govern society: "do to others as you would have them do to you". Have you never heard of the "Eleventh Commandment"? Do to others as they would do to you, only do it first?

A. Yes, that sums up the morality of our capitalist society neatly and fully. But isn't the other idea — do to others as you would like people to do to you — far better? More desirable? More in line with full human nature, which is capable of so much more than preying or trying to prey on your neighbour? For instance, every decent, sane, well-bred person has an instinctive wish to protect and nourish small children, see to their well-being, and facilitate their growth. Why shouldn't the supremely benign human impulse of healthy human adults towards small children be generalised to all people? Why couldn't it be developed and trained and extended to humanity in general? In fact it is often generalised in that way, for example in face of natural disasters and train or plane accidents. Look at the way Americans rallied to the victims of Hurricanes Harvey and Irma in 2017.

B. Human beings, developing, growing, rely on the instinct that best serves them in order to guard and protect themselves, and allows them to develop their potential.

A. Yes, but in the given conditions, and only to the extent those conditions allow.

B. Conditions developed by history, which can't be changed at will.

A. No, not at will, nor instantly by legislative change. But they can be changed. The proof is that they are changed, all the time. Socialism is also a program of how society can be changed by those who make it up, changed deliberately and systematically over time, over a period of development and refinement. The overthrow of our super-predators, the bourgeoisie, is only the start of that process. The *essential* start.

B. But it can go wrong.

A. Capitalism goes wrong! Horrendously wrong. German capitalists bred Nazism and empowered it when they felt they needed it to defend themselves against socialist revolution.

The tremendously different socio-economic formations over the last seven thousand years or more; the many different forms taken, for instance, by the family in history; and the social moralities that went with them: those all rested on the basis of one human nature. It is a malleable human nature, a human nature of which different aspects, possibilities, can be fostered, developed, made to be dominant, encouraged, or discouraged or stamped on at different times. History proves that there is no such thing as one human nature; rather, if you want to put it that way, there are many "human natures", differing in their manifest characteristics according to the refraction and conditioning in and by the different socio-economic frameworks.

The "human nature" of those who ran Hitler's concentration camps and of the Allied soldiers who liberated the inmates in 1945, choking in horror and indignation as they did so, was, on the biological and instinctual level, the same human nature. One of the things that haunts my imagination about the Nazi horrors is the fact that the people who ran the camps were sometimes in their private lives decent family men, fond and sentimental to their own children and cherishing them — in the intervals between selecting for murder, and murdering, other children, women, and men.

B. Ah, but which was predominant, the private lives of the butchers, or the butchering public lives of those who were good parents to their own children?

A. Both, at different times and circumstances, in different socially approved roles, within the space of a single day. The monstrous Mr Hyde could revert to being the sane and benign Dr Jekyll — and Dr Jekyll could become Mr Hyde again. The point is that people with the same human nature could be both the one and the other. If the demonic Nazi regime had not licensed, encouraged, fomented, and rewarded the bestiality, they would have lived out their lives, almost all of them, surely, as peaceful clerks and mundane administrators. Would Adolf Eichmann have been what he was if the German government had not licensed, employed, paid, promoted, and encouraged him? The difference was in the traits of human nature brought out and encouraged and set to work in different systems. That is the difference between socialism and capitalism. Socialism aims to create social conditions and a social morality that will cherish, reward, and develop the benign, solidarising elements and potentials of our instinctual "human nature".

The Grunwick strike in north-west London, 1976-8, saw women migrant workers take the lead and win solidarity from the settled labour movement. The mural below commemorates the Cable Street mobilisation of 1936, when workers blocked the path of Oswald Mosley's fascists to the Jewish East End

The National Health Service

A. OK, let's get down to cases in contemporary Britain. What do you think of the NHS?
B. What's that got to do with anything?
A. The battle between "socialism" and market capitalism, in which we skirmish here with words, is being fought out in life in the NHS.
B. Now you are being silly!
A. For the sake of argument, how do you see the NHS?
B. I see the NHS the way most people do. Undoubtedly a good thing.
A. And the way it has been undermined, tunnelled-under, sapped, and set up to "collapse"?
B. Has it? I don't know what you are talking about.
A. The internal market, contracting-out, cuts, and so on.
B. Necessary reforms, ensuring value for money; necessary and worthwhile economies, knitting it properly into the market system.
A. But you accept the anti-market principle of the NHS set up by the Labour government and Nye Bevan, in 1948 — medical care for everyone, free at the point of delivery?
B. Well, yes. Probably the only good thing a Labour government ever did!
A. Even now, after all the changes, and despite the cost of prescribed medicines, the NHS is still a socialist or quasi-socialist island in a capitalist sea.
B. Health care is a special case, demanding special measures.
A. Why is it a special case? And if it is a special case in Britain, why not in, say, America, where lack of health care for those who cannot pay has long been an enormous disgrace on US society — an outrage!
B. The US has its own ethos, its own way of doing things.
A. Or not doing things... It has an ultra-capitalist ethos of "the market is the one true god" and "the advertising agencies are its prophets". So, though you approve of the NHS, you wouldn't advocate a British style NHS for the USA?
B. No. Things could be improved, I suppose, but...
A. Things are being worsened in Britain now by the internal market. Without a good NHS, vast numbers in Britain would fall out of health care when they need it, as in America.
B. That's life!
A. That's death, often — if you can't pay, if you do not have insurance,

or enough insurance. If you think about it, that's the greatest inequality imaginable, the inequality between the healthy and the sick, between the living and the dying.

B. It's a natural inequality. Nothing you can do about it. Or do you think that socialism will abolish physical decrepitude and death?

A. You can treat ill-health with state-of-the-art medical care. You can't abolish death, but you can fight it, you can fend it off, and you can enable many people to live in good health who would otherwise languish in permanent pain and impairment or die early. Without a proper health-care system — "socialised medicine" — a vast amount of needless suffering and avoidable early death is our lot. Millions of babies all over the world die for lack of medicine because their parents can't afford it, and, very often, for lack of adequate food, because the parents can't afford that either.

B. It's a case of the glass half-full or half-empty. Think of the vast numbers saved and nurtured.

A. What that makes me think of is all the dead babies, all the avoidable sufferings and needless deaths, unpardonable because they are unnecessary. We have a choice. The problem is not uncontrollable raw nature, or uncontrollable diseases — though there are as yet uncontrollable diseases — but the paucity or withholding of available medical modifications of nature. Those people could be saved.

B. Maybe. But we don't live in an ideal world. We can't.

A. But we can change it! In medicine, we do that all the time. The 1948 NHS changed things radically for most people. In Britain now capitalist politicians are working to make the world a great deal less ideal — by undermining the NHS, with the longer-term objective of breaking it up. The Tory party has never put that to the electorate. Polls consistently show that a big majority favour the NHS.

B. You're imagining things. The Tories are not trying to break up the NHS!

A. They push to create and extend internal market relations — selling and buying between different parts of the NHS — and to contract out more and more of the service to private companies, at greatly increased cost, by the way! They push, manoeuvre, manipulate, and do things stealthily and bit by bit which will destroy the NHS. Bit by bit they are working to increase the inequalities, to make people even less equal than they are now, with the NHS. The neo-Thatcherites of the Blair-Brown "Labour" governments continued what the Tories began.

B. The NHS is safe with the Tories!

A. Suppose for the sake of argument that it isn't. If the Tories go openly for breaking up the NHS, and creating a two or three tier system of health care, with the poor in the bottom tier, will you be against that?

B. You're going to say that if I am against it, therefore I'm a socialist?

A. No, you are a socialist — sort of! -- just for a "special case". Only, so to speak, an episodic, "conjunctural" sort of socialist.

B. Thanks — that takes a weight off my mind.

A. Why is health the only "special case"?

B. That's obvious!

A. I mean, why not other fundamental things? Why not social housing, for instance? Why not food? Why not everything basic? Right now, isn't education another special case? Or do you think children should be unable to get a good schooling unless their parents can pay? Of course you don't.

B. Of course I don't. But health care is special. Other sectors, maybe excepting education, aren't.

A. The implication of breaking up the NHS, of "rationing" essential medicine by ability to pay, of moving to a situation like that in the USA and other places, is that the sick poor are not considered equal to the better-off and the rich. Your chance of life and health depends on how much money you have. That's an attack on everything you as a democrat claim to believe.

B. Resources are limited.

A. There are vast resources! Some could be re-channelled from the rich to the NHS. Not doing that means that those without money are sometimes now excluded from the best medicine society can offer. In Britain, to mess up the NHS (and ultimately to abolish it and replace it by a fully "market-ruled medicine") is to push people out of adequate health care. It is an obscenity. It is a direct assault, on the most fundamental level, on the idea of human equality.

B. But people aren't equal, you fool!

A. Under the NHS, in terms of health care, people in Britain were made equal, more or less. Not the same, but equal, or more equal, in the chance of life and good health. That limited equality is being destroyed. The only way it could be done, given mass support for the NHS, was piece by piece, stealthily, unacknowledgedly. What they are doing to the NHS, sapping and undermining it, flies in the face of even your democracy. It's an obscenity! And it's pluto-democracy in action!

B. It's common sense.

A. It embodies and makes explicit the reality of human inequality. As the old song has it: "If life were a thing that money could buy, then the rich would live and the poor would die".

B. Nothing you can do about it!

A. There's a lot we can do about it! Equality in health care was created by working-class political action via the post-war Labour government. It can be defended and extended by working-class action. We'll show you.

B. Dream on! If you want equality in health care, buy yourself a good private insurance scheme.

A. And if I can't afford it?

B. Tough!

The strike by women machinists at the Ford Dagenham car factory in 1968, though formally over regrading rather than equal pay, gave a huge boost to the demand for equal pay and to the revival of the women's movement in Britain.

The cover of the program pamphlet, written by Rosa Luxemburg, of the new-born German Communist Party (Spartacus League) in 1919, presents the party as fighting "new militarism", capitalism, and landlordism.

The fall of the Berlin Wall, 1989. The banner says: "For a Berlin without a wall, in a Germany without tanks, in a Europe without borders"

Part 3: The working class and socialism

The Working Class

B. The working class? The "proletariat"? Ha! That is the best example of the falseness and foolishness running through your pretended "objectivity" and the allegedly "scientific" character of your Marxist socialism! Your view of the working class is absurd.

A. Someone, John Maynard Keynes, I think it was, once asked why he should look to the social equivalent of mud, the working class, as saviour against the educated ruling classes. Why should he look for social salvation to the most ignorant, the least accomplished, the least able class in the society — to its human beasts of burden? To its "vocal tools" (as the ancient Romans described their slaves)?

B. Why indeed? You want a solution to what you call the economic and social contradictions of capitalism — and you make it a precondition of that solution that your proles should first, within this society, rise above it, above the best educated in the society. It is absurd. It is rank sentimentality — or transmuted Christianity, with its cult of the humble — on the part of middle-class socialists. In working-class socialists like you it is ridiculous narcissism. Socialists from working-class backgrounds, above all, should know better. Working-class quiescence now shows that most workers know it too.

A. Yes, the unreadiness of the working class to do in history what it alone can do is one of the basic contradictions in advanced — not to say senile! — capitalist society. We have to overcome it if society is to go forward. Other solutions, reactionary, regressive, ruinous solutions, are possible too. The Thatcherite solution was possible from the 1980s because of the political failure of the powerful working class movement of the 1970s to settle accounts, properly and finally, with the ruling class.

B. Looking to the working class is whimsical and arbitrary. It shows up the hopelessness of the socialism you espouse. That is your version of what in others you call utopian socialism. It is deeply senseless and foolish. Look at the history of the 20th century, for Christ's sake!

A. A lot less absurd than looking to the ruling class, as you do, like the snob Keynes, if you should want to change anything. To those who as a social group are tied, hand, foot, mind, and morality, to the existing system? Those who have in the 20th century resorted to Hitler, Mussolini, Peron, Chiang Kai Shek, Pinochet, and all their many similars, to stop the workers reorganising society? That strikes me as the ultimate foolishness. That is the real equivalent of the utopian romantic socialists of the early 19th century, such as the immensely great Robert Owen in Britain, appealing to the upper classes and the rich to rescue the wage slaves of capitalism and create a fair society. That is, by expropriating their class and themselves — collectively cutting their own throats. Or of the confused post-Trotsky neo-Trotskyists who in "open letters" appealed at various times in the 20th century to Stalinist dictators like Mao and Tito to abolish Stalinist rule, or to "democratise" it, which, for them, would mean the same thing as abolishing it.

B. Exactly! That is why socialism is an impossibility, an ever-shifting mirage.

A. The ruling class as a class — or its majority, or even a sizeable minority of it — will never want, initiate, or peacefully agree to an egalitarian reorganisation of society. There is an impassable barrier to that: deep-rooted self-interest. There is no such barrier to the working class wanting it. And eventually winning it, by defeating the ruling class. Not only is there no objective barrier. There is a strong incentive for working-class people to want socialism. Leaving aside maybe sections of society that have been pauperised and pushed into long-term unemployment, the working class finds no class in society lower than itself. It can exploit no-one. It must own the means of production in order to emancipate itself from the position of a class forced to sell its labour-power in order to exist. It can only own the means of production collectively — and, therefore, only democratically — because it has no way to own and administer except to do it collectively. The barriers to the working class achieving this are many. It must first come to understand the need for it and think it possible to win — that is, it must break through the domination in its minds of the ideas of the ruling class and the habit of seeing capitalist society as normal and the only possible system. It must organise and educate itself, and defeat the ruling class — a ruling class armed as it always is with every sort of weapon, from propaganda and brainwashing to the regular armies of the bourgeois state and, in acute crises, its auxiliary shock troops such as fascist thugs.

B. A tall order! An impossibility, in fact.

A. A tall order indeed! But it is not an impossibility, like the idea of the capitalist class transforming capitalism into a system without its chronic contradictions is. It can be done. That isn't just blind faith or socialist wish-thinking. We know for sure that it can be done because it has been done, most importantly in Russia in 1917.

The fundamental fact of capitalism is that it exploits the workers. The workers, in the process of working for a wage, create new value greater than the cost of their wage. This so-named "surplus value" becomes the property of the capitalist who controls the enterprise. That happens whether the worker receives high or low wages. The worker is robbed.

In turn, the capitalists are forced to compete with each other to squeeze and grind as much surplus as possible out of the workers. The most successful can grow, re-equip, and make themselves more profitable. Those who fall behind in competition are gobbled up by their successful competitors.

B. That's too fatalistic and too cynical. Even the worst people, and I don't say that they are, can be reformed. Bad systems can be reformed. The Britain we have was shaped by many reforms.

A. Reforms forced through by the revolt or pressure of the working people — for instance the revolt that created the Labour landslide in 1945, from which came the modern welfare state. That didn't come from the pure good will of the capitalist rulers, though a lot of bourgeois people had had their opposition to radical reform undermined by experience in the two World Wars (and thus you got pre-Thatcher "One Nation Toryism"). No matter how good-willed or good-intentioned a capitalist may be, or would like to be, he or she is locked into this competitive system. The rule is: exploit, accumulate wealth, expand — or die. Be predator or prey. The profit drive is therefore the all-controlling mainspring, regulator, and determinant in the system. That will remain so until conscious, democratic, overall planning replaces profit and competition as the mainspring — until the workers who are now the basic exploited class take collective ownership and substitute free cooperation for "wage slavery". Capitalist exploitation also, by its very nature, integrates workers into large collective workforces; generates constant conflicts between workers and capitalists over working hours, pay, and conditions; and pushes workers towards organising for those conflicts. We educate ourselves about politics and society in the process.

B. That credo of unreconstructed socialists and Marxists like you —

the stupid fetish of the working class — is a self-stupefying, brain-pickling dogma! I repeat: it is simply absurd.

A. And what is your unwillingness to see the working class as it really is in history? It is a great history of day-to-day struggle, heroic drives to build trade unions, general strikes, insurrections. Of course, there are also periods, sometimes long periods, of working-class passivity in the aftermath of defeats and pyrrhic victories — that is, seeming, but unreal and empty, victories like the one we won over the Tories in the mid-70s, only to have the Labour government we put into office demobilise the working-class movement and thus clear the way for Thatcher and her demolition-squad Toryism.

B. Defeated, or part-defeated, always. Always. Yes! For ever and ever, amen. Good!

A. Yes. Defeats go with the territory. Rosa Luxemburg spoke the truth when she summed it up. The socialist revolution "is the only form of 'war'... in which the ultimate victory can be prepared only by a series of 'defeats'. What does the entire history of socialism and of all modern revolutions show us? The first spark of class struggle in Europe, the revolt of the silk weavers in Lyon in 1831, ended with a heavy defeat; the Chartist movement in Britain ended in defeat; the uprising of the Parisian proletariat in the June days of 1848 ended with a crushing defeat; and the Paris Commune ended with a terrible defeat.

"The whole road of socialism — so far as revolutionary struggles are concerned — is paved with nothing but thunderous defeats. Yet, at the same time, history marches inexorably, step by step, toward final victory! Where would we be today without those 'defeats', from which we draw historical experience, understanding, power and idealism?... We stand on the foundation of those very defeats; and we can not do without any of them, because each one contributes to our strength and understanding".

B. She should know, with her poor silly head smashed in!

A. She knew it from the history of the workers' movement. We know it from history, including the defeat of the German communists in 1919 and the murder of Luxemburg, Liebknecht, Jogiches, and thousands of others. We know it from the defeat of the Bolsheviks and the working class in Russia by the Stalinist counter-revolution. Class-struggle socialists, who try to be the memory of the working class, know it all too well. There is no denying that the working class and its political movements have to operate under very unfavourable conditions.

B. Against an insuperable enemy!

A. Not an insuperable enemy. A formidable, strong, tenacious, resourceful, unscrupulous enemy, which has enormous built-in advantages, great political guile, and immense reserves of strength. That enemy has all the wealth. It has control of the propaganda and education machines in society. It has the power and wealth to buy over some of our people. I think it was the Liberal Imperialist Joseph Chamberlain who sneered to the Fabian Beatrice Webb, about working-class trade-union and political leaders: "You train them, and we'll buy them".

B. Exactly! Your whole project is hopeless and ridiculous. You are hypnotising yourself! Look around you! All around you is the evidence of working-class defeat and indifference — sensible indifference! — to your message and your cause. You believe far more preposterous things than the Christians, Muslims, Jews and other such self-hypnotising addicts of religious fairy stories for grown-ups, whom you mock and deride. You believe that a too-often defeated class can be victorious at some unknown future time. That is a tall tale for immature adults who can't come to terms with social reality. The future belongs to the working class? Yes, and the dead will get up and walk the streets on an appointed day! And the trumpet will sound to announce the imminence of the kingdom of God on earth! You believe in miracles.

A. Not quite. There is a rational basis for our "miracles". Dead men and women don't get up and walk. In society, defeated classes do rise again.

In all societies and in all history, the basic exploited class revolts. Revolts again and again. In our history, the working class has risen from defeat again and again and again. That is the other side of the defeats. Every victory of the bourgeoisie is incomplete. It can't win outright, because it needs to preserve the working class to do the work. Even while British capitalism was defeating the British working class in the 1980s, capitalism was vastly increasing the number of workers in other areas of the world. Capitalism creates its own legions of gravediggers — the proletariat.

B. It is its own grave that the "proletariat" digs! Again and again and again. And a good thing too!

A. Don't let that wish father foolish thoughts on you! The long history of the working class, of its defeats, its declines, and its revivals, shows us what will happen in the future, though not of course in exact detail. It is sure and certain that working-class struggle will revive and rise much higher than it is now. The working-class socialist movement will revive.

Everything in history shows us that it will. Why? Because capitalism can live only by exploiting the "labour force", and workers fight back, if only on a trade-union level at first. There are many working-class struggles around the world now. We, the working-class socialists, will build new working-class political parties, on the foundations of working-class struggle and of the lessons of our history.

B. Yeah, and Atlantis will rise again! And you will get sense...

A. The Atlantis of legend never existed. But even the legends offer us good advice... Atlantis was where the Minoan civilisation of Crete and Homeric Greece was supposed to have come from, borne by survivors — as socialists now bear socialist culture and historical awareness for the future.

B. Minoan socialism! Not "scientific" socialism, but myth-mounted socialism! A socialist Theseus lost in the capitalist maze! I like it.

A. The history of working-class mobilisation, struggle, sustained effort, prolonged resistance, outright revolt — that is neither myth nor merely legend! It could be argued, on the basis of the numerous working-class revolts in history, back to the seizure of the city of Lyons in 1831 and beyond, that the working class has a *will to* power, albeit a fluctuating one.

B. There may have been big, threatening, socialist movements in the past, but you can't win now.

A. We'll see. Naturally I have no guarantees to offer to you, or to those attracted to socialism, about exactly when the working class will revive, or when or where it will next be victorious.

And I am not saying that we should wait for the working class to revive on a world scale before we can do anything. I do say that the full solution — the creation of a world-wide democratically-planned economy controlled by those who work it — can only be achieved by the working class. Humankind will not sink into passive acceptance of injustice, inequality, and rampant rule-by-the-rich. Beyond that, it is a fight; right now, a battle on what someone called "the ideological front" (as distinct from the political and economic fronts of the class struggle).

The one thing that is certain is that the working-class struggle on its lower or higher levels will go on, as it is going on now — and that serious socialists will work to help those fighting in that struggle to find their way through the political and ideological mazes of capitalism.

B. The fact that you admit that you can offer no guarantees shows how confident you really are in your expectations and predictions.

A. It shows that I know the limits of my own or anyone else's power to predict in detail, to know in advance the strength of our enemies, the obstacles we must overcome, the complexities and intractabilities of history. And, therefore, that I am not a charlatan or a megalomaniac.

B. Are you sure? But, really, look at the historical record. When you demand, as you do, miraculous changes in attitudes and moralities — and first of all from the wretched "proletariat" — is it any wonder that socialists have not succeeded?

A. It is not a matter of miracles. We build on what already exists in society and in the working class. Inside capitalism, the labour movement has always been and is now a repository of values other than those of the surrounding society — of the values of class and human solidarity. Characteristically we have argued, for example, for changing environments that produce crime rather than severely punishing criminals. Trade unions fight the capitalists for a better share of what the workers produce, or to stop the workers' share being diminished. They fight on bread-and-butter questions to benefit the workers. But in the trade unions you will also find tremendous stores of benevolence, altruism, fellow-feeling, selfless devotion to the common good. Workers sacrifice wages to their spirit of solidarity with other workers. The drive to change things for the better triggered by the elemental "trade union" struggle over the effects of capitalism tends to nourish the manifold values of solidarity. Not perfectly and instantly; but the contrast between the labour movement and the society around it is always one between greater civilisation, greater humanity, greater solidarity, and a more predatory culture. We build on that, just as we build our perspective on the inner logic of capitalism's own development.

B. You *want* it to be so, that I understand. What you want is impossible. Foolishness! Dreaming! Dangerous dreaming that might again damage what we have now.

A. Only those who actively and perseveringly want such changes can bring them about. But the fact that such things have happened before is a proof that they can be made to happen again. Because mass socialist labour movements have been built before, they can be built again. Or, putting it at its weakest, there is no absolute reason why such movements can't be built again, in conditions which have changed in many ways but are the same in fundamentals — capitalist exploitation; working-class resistance to it; the socialising drives, tendencies, and needs of capital itself, and the educational work of socialists.

Labour movements can be, and, I say, will be again converted to socialism, which is the natural expression of what the working class is, and the necessary negation of the capitalist class and its system.

B. Those mass socialist labour movements were crushed and defeated. You know that. They have gone the way that other such would-be benevolent schemes have gone. All in all, I say that is a good thing.

A. What hasn't "gone" is capitalism, its modes of operating, and the effects it produces in working-class people. It is capitalism that breeds socialism! In the socialist seeding time is the class struggle. The wolves running wild in society evoke class and human solidarity in self-protection and in revolt and revulsion against them and their wolvish system.

B. It is easy to say all that. It has no purchase on reality.

A. No? Take the experience of the Labour Party. At its best it was a reform-socialist party. The Blair-Brown coup of 1994, backed by some union leaders, made the Labour Party a neo-Thatcherite party. It ruled as a neo-Thatcherite party from 1997 to 2010. Since 2015 it has revived as a party of the working class and of reform socialism. British politics is being transformed. We have a long way to go yet. We may experience setbacks. But Labour could change, "miraculously", because vast numbers of people felt the need for it. Revolutionary socialism will revive, too.

Platinum miners in South Africa protest against the shooting of dozens of their workmates by South African police during a pay strike in 2012. The strikers nevertheless won large wage rises and consolidated their militant union.

Working-Class Solidarity

A. People have motivations for action other than crude direct self-interest, certainly motivations other than monetary self-interest. Motives of class, social, and human solidarity, of doing good to other people, of benign sharing and being shared with, of being part of a benign collective, and simply of being a decent human being.

In Britain before Thatcher you used to see that a lot in industrial disputes. Workers would lose wages rather than cross a picket line, that is, rather than sabotage other workers in their efforts to better themselves. More than once, other workers, coal-miners for instance, struck on behalf of hospital workers who were inhibited in taking action by the dependence on them of sick people.

You see that spirit in people responding to accidents and to the needs of accident victims. In war, people often sacrifice themselves for their comrades. You still see that spirit in industrial disputes now.

B. These are all atypical, extreme, freakish cases. The norm is what you denounce as the epitome of capitalism: enlightened self-interest.

A. In the most thoroughly capitalist-minded society in the world, the USA, between 25% and 30% of all people over 16 do organised voluntary work, a total of eight billion hours a year, and over 75% of them do informal voluntary work to help neighbours or friends.

B. God, what a stupid sentimentalist you are!

A. Am I? Isn't it that you are a stupid misanthrope? That you have a perversely one-sided idea of the nature of human beings and of our possibilities? Here it is a question of the way real people behave, as distinct from your malign model of all-consuming selfishness. What you are saying is a libel on humankind. Your attitude to humankind is bred in you by the worst aspects of present-day human society. You are psychologically maimed, though you'd be the last to know it.

B. Bred in me by the realities of the world as it is, always has been, and always will be. And your attitudes and ideals? Bred in you, most likely, by over-indulgent parents!

A. And you? I bet you were beaten, sent to bed without your supper, and locked in dark cupboards! Your parents probably gave you stingy pocket money and then made you pay for the meals you ate in their internal-market family economy! Probably charged you separately for the use of a corner of their table and the chair you sat on. And for the use of cutlery and condiments!

B. At least I didn't grow up wet with sticky, false sentimentality.

A. Certainly the culture we live in, and the ideals and heroes held up to society, are nearly all now of the predator-or-prey, the be-the-hammer-or-be-the-anvil type you describe. That can change. In fact it can change quickly. Take an example from working-class history: the port workers, dockers.

B. Must we?

A. Ships come, discharge their cargo, load another cargo, and go. There is no continuity of work in such conditions. For a long time, thousands of years, I guess, gangs of dock workers would be sent when needed to hump cargo on and off ships. Entry into the work was unregulated. Anyone could turn up for a job on the docks. It was a buyer's market in labour. Workers would compete with each other to get hired for half a day's work. They would crowd around the hiring foreman, and sometimes fight each other for preference. The big and burly men could push the weaker men aside. The foremen would pay wages in pubs — getting a cut from the landlords for it — so men would drink there. It was the social Darwinist's dream, or nightmare — a world of dog-eat-dog individualism and the survival of the strongest. The weakest went down and were trampled, sometimes literally trampled, underfoot. The men were wolves fighting wolves, dogs fighting dogs, for scraps. Then at the end of the 1880s the British dockers formed a union, with the help of socialists like Tom Mann and John Burns, who were not dockers but skilled engineers, and Eleanor Marx. Dockers still competed with dockers for jobs, but the docks were radically transformed, from a system and an ethos of every-man-for-himself to an all-shaping culture of working-class solidarity. The dockers learned the power they had when they stood together, and how much better it was when each docker looked out for himself by looking out for the others too.

B. Holding the country to ransom! In fact, being pig-selfish.

A. You, who lauded capitalist greed a moment ago, think you can now denounce "pig-selfishness" in workers fighting for a living wage!

B. I detest your sentimentalism, your idealisation of the lower depths of society.

A. And I detest your snobbery! Your ridiculous self-blinding snobbery. A Royal Commission of inquiry on the ports in 1965 reported that dockers' solidarity was such that it only needed one docker running down a quay on which a line of ships were being worked, shouting the news that men on one ship, or in one warehouse, had a grievance and had stopped work, and all the others would come out in solidarity. That was the truth.

A generation or so after the 1889 docks strike and the start of unionisation, the old culture had been turned upside down and inside out. Dockers used solidarity as a weapon in the never-ending strife with the bosses, and learned to hold up social solidarity as a socialist ideal to work for in politics.

As a dockworker in the 1960s, I saw and took part in things that have sustained my belief in the working class, and what it can and will do, through decades of working-class defeat and retreat.

B. Shhh… Don't boast about your own stupidity! Your point in the here and now is what? That culture, if it really was as you say, has vanished. It doesn't exist any more. It didn't have much vitality then, did it?

A. It had great vitality. We were defeated, after big and prolonged conflicts.

B. Good! In any case, that culture proved unviable, again and again.

A. Or take the town labourers in my home town, Ennis, in the west of Ireland. In this farmers' market town which was also the administrative centre of County Clare, a place with schools and colleges and many teachers, priests and nuns, the town labourers were dirt. We lived in what were officially and routinely, in County Medical Officers' reports, called "hovels". Many were illiterate. They were semi-outcasts to be hired as needed and then jettisoned to their regular condition of being half-starved. They relied for survival on big extended families that cared and shared for each other. And then, learning I guess from the example of the tenant farmers' "trade union", the Land League, they organised a trade union, a one-town union five or six hundred strong. Soon the labourers, banded together, showed that solidarism can replace dog-eat-dog-ism. They stood by each other — walked off jobs they sorely needed to act in support of their fellow trade unionists. It was very like the culture on the docks. It was magnificent.

B. Mugs! At best a small footnote to history.

A. It was like that in other, similar, towns, such as Kilrush, for example. That sort of working-class solidarity had tremendous vitality, and, in many places and over spans of many decades.

B. What happened to it?

A. In Ennis, World War 2 pulled the labourers to migrate. In the ports, there was a radical technological revolution. Giant containers were loaded away from the docks and delivered there ready to be moved by cranes from the trucks or railway wagons to the ships. Incoming containers were lifted off ships by cranes to lorries or railway wagons. That was the precondition for everything. The tremendously militant dockers were defeated by bosses' governments, Labour as well as Conservative. So was the whole working class defeated in the 1980s. The class struggle sometimes boils up, sometimes subsides from exhaustion, or after working-class defeat. But the class struggle is a fundamental fact of social life. It always exists, at a higher level or at a lower. It always revives after defeats. The impulse to working-class solidarity is there still. It will make itself felt again.

B. They were beaten — and what makes you think they won't always be beaten? I've heard and read about the way things were in Britain before Margaret Thatcher came to power — the so-named "Winter of Discontent". Striking dust-cart workers and striking gravediggers left rubbish piled in the streets and dead bodies unburied. Those workers deserved what they got from Thatcher! She saved Britain from the wreckers.

A. Yes. She and her government had to wreck Britain in order to save it from the trade-unionist "wreckers"! A real heroine, that one. By the way, the "unburied bodies" is Tory spin-liar stuff, with a slim basis of fact.

Hungarian workers topple a statue of Stalin during the 1956 revolution

Radical Decline of The Working Class?

B. In any case, your cherished working class is diminishing. It is now too weak to revolutionise society or anything else.

A. The opposite is true. Now is probably the first time in history that the wage-workers and their immediate families are the largest class in the population of the world.

According to the International Labour Organisation, the world's waged workforce increased from 0.9 billion in 1991 to 1.7 billion in 2014. Even though a large number of those, in the poorer countries, are "semi-proletarians", who scrape a living by varying combinations of petty trade, self-employment, theft, begging, domestic work, and straightforward wage-work, the actual number of wage-workers has increased sharply.

B. But that's not the real working class, manual workers in factories.

A. Your idea of "working class" is far too narrow. The working class is not only manual workers. It never has been. What defines workers is their relation to capital. This is how Marx put it: "With the development of... the specifically capitalist mode of production, the real lever of the overall labour process is increasingly not the individual worker. Instead, labour-power socially combined and the various competing labour-powers which together form the entire production machine participate in very different ways... one as a manager [Marx means a low-level administrator or organiser], engineer, technologist, etc., the other as overseer, the third as manual labourer or even drudge... It is quite immaterial whether the job of a particular worker, who is merely a limb of this aggregate worker, is at a greater or smaller distance from the actual manual labour".

B. Teachers, technicians, and so on — they're middle class.

A. No, they are part of the working class.

B. Most of them would say you are wrong.

A. Most manual workers in the USA call themselves "middle class". Such labels don't change their place in the economy, or the way they relate to the hirer of their labour-power, the capitalist. Whatever they choose to call themselves, they are what Marx called the proletariat. They are working-class.

B. A "class" as diverse as the working class now is can never unite. Inequalities in wages and living standards have increased since the early 1980s within the working class as well as between the working class and the capitalist class.

A. That diversity is not new either, though of course you'll believe what you want to believe. Inequalities within the working class were large in Marx's day too. The central divide remains the one between the working class and the capitalist class. That is not diminishing!

B. Better-off workers share more with what you call the petty bourgeoisie than with the working class. The worse-off workers are a minority in society. Any politics which appeals only to them cannot succeed. And in any case your socialist ideas have little support even among them.

A. We don't confine our appeal to the worst-off sections of the working class. Or even only to the working class. A mass socialist labour movement would have a wider appeal, even beyond the working class properly defined. You are also mistaken in your sociology of the working class. There is a fundamental difference between better-off workers and the "petty bourgeoisie". You can see it in the fact that the small business owner or the "middle manager" votes much more right-wing than the teacher or nurse well up on their pay scale.

B. You are flamming to yourself, fooling yourself, using political voting allegiances instead of the proper economic and social criteria.

A. The social and economic difference between better-off workers and the petty bourgeoisie remains enormous. For instance, in times of higher class struggle, the well-off workers are drawn into (and quite often they lead) the general workers' struggle; the petty bourgeois are still petty bourgeois.

B. The relative decline of factory labour cuts away what you see as the revolutionary potential of the working class.

A. It does not cut it away, though it may relocate it to a certain extent. Certain sections of the working class have greater strategic weight than others: those who directly produce the bulk of socially-useful products, those who can hit capital hardest, those who are concentrated in big workplaces and large cities, those most bitterly hurt by capitalist exploitation. Shop-floor workers in factories and in extractive industry are central — but also warehouse workers, goods-transport workers, and those in such sectors as post and telecom, and maybe even bank workers or teachers. The factory working class is still much larger than in Marx's or Lenin's day. It has expanded fast on a world scale in recent decades, even though it shrank a bit in the older industrial countries, and has now begun to shrink in new industrial countries too.

B. It is not what Marx expected to happen, is it?

A. Isn't it? Your Marx is a "Marx" for the superficial and shoddy polemicist. You are simply wrong to think that Marx saw a population almost all made up of factory workers. Marx's own analysis of the English census of 1861 showed only 1.7 million workers in factories, mines, gasworks, and railways, out of a population of 20 million.

B. Yes, but Marx saw the numbers of industrial workers as increasing, and they did up to, say, World War One. Not now.

A. In Germany, the country Marxists cited as the epitome of high capitalist development around World War One, 34% of the labour force were self-employed or working for their families. Capitalist society is more "proletarianised" now than then in the fundamental sense of the proportion of people drawn into the capital-labour nexus, who live by selling their labour-power.

B. But students are middle-class!

A. Even here you are wrong. It is no longer accurate to call students, as a social category, "middle class". Many of them come from working-class families (usually better-off), and will go into (usually better-paid) wage-labour on finishing their studies. Students are a fluid social group without clear class anchoring. They can be a vital leaven for democratic struggles and even sometimes for socialist struggles.

Shipyard workers in Gdansk at the time of the birth of Solidarnosc in 1980. Before it was pushed back by state repression and lack of solidarity from the workers' movement in Western Europe, Solidarnosc defined its aim as a "self-managing society"

Stonebreakers on the side of the road outside Ennis, County Clare, in the late 30s or early 40s. All of these men will have been members of the Ennis United Labourers' Union (p.57). Below: Wilhelm Liebknecht, joint founder of the SPD, and his son Karl Liebknecht.

Part 4: Socialism, Democracy, and Stalinism

Is It Either Public Ownership or Democracy?

B. Didn't Stalinism do what socialists advocated? Didn't it "nationalise" the economy? Statify it? You say that "socialism" is what you say it is, and not what everyone else says it is!

A. Would you accept your politics being equated with all those who call themselves "right-wing" or "conservative"? You wouldn't. The truth is that the self-definition of the left, in capitalist society, is always and inevitably a struggle against rabid misrepresentation and unreasoning prejudice. And even more so now, after Stalin.

B. The leftists who see future socialism as a perhaps modified version of what you call Stalinism have logic and common sense on their side. Those 20th century socialist states...

A. Stalinist states!

B. ... had what even you see as the main content of socialism, state ownership of the main means of production.

A. Do you seriously think that for socialists nationalisation is socialism, irrespective of everything else in society? Of who rules in society? It isn't. It never was. It can't be. What do you think those who made the Russian Revolution believed? In common with all Marxists then, they believed:

"State ownership and control is not necessarily socialism — if it were, then the Army, the Navy, the police, the judges, the gaolers, the informers, and the hangmen, all would all be socialist functionaries, as they are state officials — but the ownership by the state of all the land and materials for labour, combined with the co-operative control by the workers of such land and materials, would be socialism... An immense gulf separates the 'nationalising' proposals of the middle class from the 'socialising' demands of the revolutionary working class. The first proposes to endow a class state... with certain powers and functions to be administered in the common interest of the possessing class; the second proposes to subvert the class state and replace it with the socialist state, representing organised society — the socialist republic.

"To the cry of the middle class reformers, 'make this or that the property of the government', we reply, 'yes, in proportion as the workers are ready to make the government their property'."

B. Who are you quoting? Lenin?

A. No, that was James Connolly, in 1899, expressing the viewpoint common to all Marxists then. Wounded in the 1916 uprising, he was propped up in a chair and shot by the British army for trying to establish the right of the Irish nation to democratic self-rule, 18 months before the October Revolution. Nationalisation without democracy and without a workers' state, so Marxist socialists thought then, would produce only the tyranny of an elite. George Plekhanov declared: "There will not be any self-government by the people and the revolution which has taken place may lead to a political monster similar to the ancient Chinese or Peruvian empires, i.e., to a renewal of tsarist despotism with a communist lining".

B. Plekhanov opposed the Bolsheviks in 1917.

A. Yes. But Trotsky was a central leader of the Bolsheviks in 1917. He wrote in 1936, of Russian "socialism": "The means of production belong to the state. But the state, so to speak, 'belongs' to the bureaucracy." In fact, the nationalisation of everything, even the street corner shops, was specific to Stalinism. It came out of the Stalinist bureaucracy's drive in a backward country to eliminate all rivalry for control of resources, of the surplus product, even that of small shopkeepers, artisans and so on. In this also Stalinism was a product of Russia's backwardness and extreme poverty.

B. Such concentration of economic, social, and political power in the hands of the state inevitably produces tyranny. You say there were people in the Russian revolution who did not like what the Russian state became? I'll admit that socialists often have good intentions. But those intentions are not realisable. The attempt to realise them will always produce tyranny.

A. Why?

B. Because widespread public ownership inevitably gives great power to those who control the government machine. They will inevitably use that power in their own interests. Democracy can exist and thrive only in an economy where ownership is dispersed. It is bound to perish where it is concentrated.

A. That doesn't augur well for the future of democracy if capitalism continues, then, does it? The big corporations are dominant, and becoming more and more dominant. Under modern capitalism, ownership is greatly concentrated and is becoming more concentrated.

B. With a free market there are always limits to that concentration. There are always new competitors.

A. But the big businesses dominate, even if from time to time one big corporation declines and another takes its place at the top. Maybe capitalist competition stops the general administration of society being dominated by a single fixed cartel of leading capitalists. Nonetheless it remains dominated by the general interests of all big business.

B. Not as completely as it would be with public ownership of all the major enterprises.

A. That depends...

B. On what exactly?

A. On democracy, or the absence of it. Your argument about the inevitability of tyranny under widespread public ownership is really an argument about democracy, an argument that democracy is impossible. Or rather, you concede that present-day parliamentary democracy is too weak to stop big-business bosses dominating affairs; you assume that no better democracy is possible; and so you "prove" to your own satisfaction that public ownership can only be bureaucratic ownership, and never democratic collective ownership. Here our differences hinge on the nature, extent, and possibilities of democracy — or, in fact, on whether a full democracy is realisable at all. Under your bluster, you have as little belief in democracy as you have ambition for its development.

B. It takes some cheek for you to say that — an advocate of the socialism which spawned 20th century totalitarianism, or of something like it!

A. Working-class socialism requires and presupposes a regime of all-pervading political, social, and economic democracy, where representatives and officials have no privileges. A system which allows everyone the same access to the means of information, and to free time for political activity. That will be a state in the process of withering away, losing its coercive tools and functions, in a functioning socialist economy, society, and polity.

B. You hope!

A. Yes, but with more than uninformed and passive hope. Socialists fight for that fuller democracy. We educate those whom we win to socialism in that democratic thought, spirit, and political program. We can and we will achieve it. It is central to our entire socialist political project.

Clockwise from top left: James Connolly; Gracchus Babeuf, who tried to organise a communist rising in the wake of the French Revolution of 1789-94 and was guillotined in 1797; Edith Lanchester (see page 33); Albert Einstein, who was a socialist as well as a scientist; Clara Zetkin, leader of the socialist women's movement in Germany before World War One, and also a leader of the left wing of the Social Democratic Party.

Stalinism In History

B. The Russian Revolution which you praise evolved more or less smoothly into Stalinism. There was no coup.

A. Vladimir Lenin, with his last dying strength, tried to remove Joseph Stalin from his lynchpin place in the organisational structures of the Communist Party and in the state. Trotsky led the Bolshevik opposition to Stalin and Stalinism. To defeat that opposition, Stalin destroyed the Bolshevik party, murdered most of its leaders and members, falsified its history, and kept its name for a system with which the real Bolshevik party and the revolution it led had nothing in common.

Trotsky fired a running Bolshevik bombardment at Stalinism for 17 years, criticising it, denouncing and damning it, and putting forward programs and strategies for the working class struggle to smash and overthrow it. Continuously, he measured its deepening degeneration against the program of the October Revolution and the Bolsheviks who led it.

He criticised the forced collectivisation and the breakneck industrialisation, the enslavement of the working class, driven like cattle by the Stalinists, the degradation of Marxism into a mere bureaucratic pidgin-religion, a system of rationalising whatever Stalin did. He tried to organise the USSR workers to make a new working-class revolution against Stalinism. He led a whole generation of Bolsheviks who fought to resist and then overthrow Stalinism. The very least any honest anti-Bolshevik can do in face of these facts is admit that something more is involved in this history than the smooth evolution of Vladimir Lenin's and Leon Trotsky's Bolshevik party into its own opposite, and its own murderer, Stalinism.

The grim joke here is that Stalinism lied and misrepresented itself and its history to claim continuity with Bolshevism — and long after European Stalinism is in its grave the bourgeoisie takes over, cherishes, nurtures, augments, updates, and disseminates this part of the legacy of Stalinism! Thieves of a feather lie together!

B. But the Trotskyists were defeated. Stalin and his friends won and they decided what happened: that's what is historically important. That is *history*! If there was a struggle within Bolshevism, and of course everybody knows that there was, the Stalinists won, and that was no accident. Stalin and his followers never ceased to call themselves socialists and Marxists and Bolsheviks, and that was what they really were.

A. I might call myself the true king of Ireland, but you wouldn't believe me if I did, would you? Bolshevism was defeated, but it did not die. Trotsky and the Opposition embodied Bolshevism counterposing itself to Stalinism and fighting it. They were leaders of both the revolution — Trotsky organised the insurrection in St Petersburg in 1917 — and of the fight to stop, destroy, undo the Stalinist counter-revolution against the working class.

B. But they did not shape what happened! Stalin developed the real-world practice and theory of 20th century socialism. Stalin re-made socialism. What Stalin did was socialism — full stop!

A. In other words, what Stalin and his successors and emulators said they were doing, or thought they were doing, when they did what they did, *made* it socialism!

B. Yes!

A. What Stalin did was socialism, because he said it was? It was Bolshevism, because he said it was? It was Marxism, because he said it was? What he did, the semi-slave society ruled by terror which he created — that was Marxist, Bolshevik Socialism, because he said it was!

Though somehow, even though he said it was democracy incarnate, that doesn't matter. That does not taint or discredit democracy. You *know*, you say, that it wasn't democracy, and that's enough.

B. Because it *wasn't* democracy.

A. It wasn't socialism, either! Who anointed Stalin Pope, who appointed him Caliph, to decide those things?

B. He anointed himself Pope! He sanctified and empowered himself. Like Napoleon Bonaparte he crowned himself. He made himself dictator and Pope of the socialist and Marxist world, and that's what counts. Stalin in his own way was a great man.

A. Yes, of course: he'd have been a great capitalist entrepreneur had he had the good fortune to be born in the USA or Britain! He'd be a billionaire. He'd be a Donald Trump! The Stalinists proclaimed themselves the only socialists — and you won't hear a word said against that proposition! If you had lived then and felt driven to be a socialist by the semi-collapse of capitalism in the 1930s...

B. God forbid!

A. ... in Stalin's time you would have been a Stalinist. God protect us from political simple-mindedness and shell-armoured ignorance! And from naked and shameless power-worship such as yours. You are hypnotised politically by the power of capitalism now. And just a little bit impressed by the once-upon-a-time power of Stalin and his clones, tools, and accomplices.

B. God protect us from people in a state of political and historical denial!

A. The Stalinists always were the bourgeoisie's ideal socialists. You and your ideological brothers and sisters still spout the lies the Stalinist state told about socialism and Marxism and Bolshevism as your version of the truth about socialism: the great lie that they were the only socialists, Marxists, Bolsheviks, Leninists. The Stalinists had one sort of use for that compound lie; you have another. In both cases you target the truth about Bolshevism, socialism, Marxism, the Russian workers' revolution. In this you are, so to speak, in a retrospective alliance with the Stalinists. You malign the memory of those who led the most democratic revolution in history, and those Bolsheviks who fought Stalin as long as they were alive. The Stalinists' lie that they were democrats — that you choose to ignore.

You use the Stalinists' anthraxed "socialism" to make the capitalists, by contrast, seem clean and healthy. Historical truth is the casualty. So is rational discussion of the socialist alternative to capitalism now.

B. Well, aren't the capitalists clean, by comparison?

A. Are they? Depends which capitalists, at which stage of capitalist development, you take. Nothing was dirtier than German capitalism under the geno-maniacal Nazis.

B. Now you are using criticism of capitalism to excuse Stalinism

A. I don't "excuse" Stalinism! Again: the real socialists and Marxists criticised and condemned the Stalinists and their crimes — from forced collectivisation at the beginning of the 1930s, through China's Cultural Revolution (from 1966), to the invasion of Afghanistan in December 1979. In the historically short time of its existence, Stalinism was worse than capitalism. I don't deny that. I deny that socialism has anything in common with those horrors. I deny that those horrors justify and exonerate capitalism.

B. Yes, of course you deny it. You have to, in order to resist the necessary logical conclusion from that terrible experience!

A. Logic! Logical reasoning needs to be a valid chain: you create an artificial chain of your own. You ignore everything that speaks against the identity of working-class socialism, Marxism, Bolshevism, and Stalinism.

B. You simply won't accept what is obvious to all sensible people: Stalinism killed socialism. First it corrupted the old socialist ideals.

They're not my ideals, but they were not entirely negligible or contemptible ideas and ideals. Then Stalinism destroyed socialism — the scorpion eating its own poisonous tail. Socialism is dead.

A. In the 20th century, Hitler, Stalin, David Ben Gurion, Clement Attlee, Fidel Castro, Leon Blum, Gamal Abdul Nasser, Saddam Hussein, Mao Zedong, Leon Trotsky, Rosa Luxemburg, Buenaventura Durruti — they all called themselves "socialists" — socialists, or Arab socialists, national socialists, Ba'th socialists, Zionist socialists, anarchist socialists, etc. All of them had a common element, of sorts, expressed in the word "socialism", namely state or social action. (The anarchist socialists believed in social but not state action). But, if they are defined by what they did, or by the doctrines they proclaimed and under whose banner they acted, or by the social classes for which they acted, then they can't all have been socialist. Say they were all socialists because they all said they were, and you reduce socialism to a meaningless word. Yes, that, I suppose, is pretty much what the 20th century itself did to the word "socialism". But it is not the end of the story.

Your glib abuse of socialism is a foolish block on perception, thought, and understanding. It works to crowd out discussion of capitalism, of what it is: a particular historical socio-economic formation, one of a number, one of a series. Whatever capitalism is, you insist, however horrible aspects of it are, there is no better alternative: Stalinism was worse, and Stalinism is the socialist alternative to capitalism. Therefore there is no real and certainly no desirable alternative.

On the level of historical fact and of serious argument it is a frame-up. Marxist socialism, communism, cannot just be sunk into a mere vague word, "socialism", and equated with what the self-named "socialists" Stalin or Mao or Hitler did in power. It cannot be made responsible for everything done by people calling themselves socialists or prefix-socialists, for example national-socialists, Ba'thist Arab socialists, Zionist socialists, etc. Marxist socialism was never just a matter of general aspirations and wishes for a better or an ideal world, such as many "socialisms" had been across the centuries as far back as classical Greece and Plato, most likely even earlier. It was never a "utopia", an ideal, arbitrary blueprint worked out in someone's head to be imposed on reality. Marxism is a thoroughly worked-out account of social history, an analysis of capitalism, of its laws of motion, its history, its tendencies, and its necessary evolution. The socialism of Marx — our socialism — was, in its analysis and its expectations from that analysis, based on the history of capitalism itself, its evolution, the concentration and socialisation of production and distribution which capitalism brings through its own development. That is still true.

B. If socialism is inevitable, if it exists, so to speak, in the "genes" of capitalist society, then why didn't it break through the barriers and give birth to itself in the 20th century?

A. Because the economic dynamic works itself out, and can only work itself out, through people — through the class struggle between the exploited, the have-nots, and the exploiters, the "haves". And we were defeated in that struggle in the 20th century. The owners dispose of great wealth and the services of many people tied to them by privileges and pay-outs. The "haves" are tied to the system that gives them wealth and the power of shaping and reshaping society now. Naturally they defend it. An individual here and there from among them may change sides in the conflict and come over to socialism, and many have done that, but this powerful and entrenched class stands like a gigantic series of rocks across the highway of history, across the logical and necessary development of humanity further along the road capitalism itself has already built, and indicates still.

B. Indicates?

A. The inner, the intrinsic, conflict of capitalist society is about how the socialised, but not yet socialist, forces of production should be operated, and for whom. For the owners' private profit, or for the good of society as a whole? This ruling class has inflicted defeat, again and again, on those who tried to resolve the contradiction between society and the private ownership of the social means of production, exchange, and communications.

Societies do not only go forward. The class struggle can lead, and in history has led, to stagnation and regression, to a lesser society — to what Marx and Engels as long ago as the Communist Manifesto of 1848 called "the mutual ruination of the contending classes". Much of the history of the 20th century is the history of the partial or temporary ruination of the contending classes: the utter ruination of Germany and other parts of Europe in the 1940s, for instance. A progressive solution to the inner conflict of capitalism requires the victory over the ruling class of the opposite group — the triumph of the non-owners of the means of production, of capitalism's main exploited class, of its "wage slaves", of the working class.

B. More double-talk. The idea of the working class as the protagonist of your socialist revolution is an idiotic mystical-religious elevation of the poor and the downtrodden and exploited in someone's well-meaning addled head.

A. The proletariat was a product of capitalism, and is so now. Around the world, there are greatly more of us now than there ever were. We say that the proletariat, the wage-labour class of people who, to live, must sell their labour-power, is historically the bearer of socialism. Why? Because it alone can resolve the contradiction within capitalism between private ownership and social-ised production. And how? By establishing collective social control, democratic control, over the production processes that knit together vast social networks. The working class will do that because it needs to free itself from exploitation and social mistreatment and from the general mismanagement of society by the buyers of labour-power, the bourgeoisie. In the French Revolution of 1789-94 and similar revolutions the land of the great landlords could be divided up by their former serfs, the peasantry. Modern industry can not be divided up like that. It can only be owned by the working class and by all the working people collectively. And that also, necessarily, means democratically.

B. So you say. But in the 20th century collective ownership meant tyranny!

A. They didn't have collective ownership. You can't have real collective ownership without democracy. I mean collective ownership by the working class, by the people. Not "collective ownership" by a small minority, by a ruling bureaucracy. Collectively-controlled economy without democracy is a contradiction in terms: either the people own collectively, and that means democratically, or it is the sham collectivism of Stalinist state ownership. As Trotsky puts it: if the state owns the economy, then the question is, who "owns" the state? Who has political power?

That is the decisive question. The working class, in aspiring to own the great enterprises produced by capitalism, can only aspire to own them collectively and thus democratically (unlike the peasants, who could divide up the land taken from the big landlords). That is why socialists who are not democrats would be and are a contradiction in terms.

B. In actual history, socialism is the enemy of democracy.

A. In the early 19th century, many would have said that in actual history, democratic republics had only produced tyrannies like Napoleon Bonaparte's; that they were the enemies of a freedom possible only with a constitutional monarchy and a right to vote restricted to a propertied minority. In the 20th century, there were regimes which called themselves "socialist", as they also called themselves "democratic", which were the enemies of democracy and of socialism. When they called themselves "socialist", they lied in order to camouflage what in fact they were. If the Stalinists, the Maoists, the Ba'thists, were "the socialists", then the socialism and communism of Marx and Lenin need another name. The eruption of those alien formations, Nazi or Stalinist, which took on the name socialist because it was popular and because in their own way and for their own ends they believed in state action, did not mean that authentic socialism sank into being just one of the variants of "socialism" or "prefix-socialism". The criticism of these political formations by their contemporary Marxist socialists is enough to establish that.

B. Evasion! You drown in your own intellectual dishonesty!

A. There is nothing evasive and no bad faith or dishonesty in taking those things into account. There is evasion, special pleading, self-blinding, and vicious know-nothing bad faith in doing what you do. You damn Marxist socialism, working-class socialism, by attributing to us the vile deeds of the most powerful groups that *called* themselves socialist or communist in the 20th century. In fact, of political formations which murdered god knows how many of us, which oppressed and even enslaved the workers, and which in no way met the criteria of working-class or Marxist socialism. Least of all the key criterion: self-liberation of the working-class.

Marxists had never said that state control of the economy, implemented by no matter whom, would bring progress. They had said the opposite. The Stalinist so-called "socialist" political formations arose in societies which lacked those economic, social, cultural, and intellectual preconditions for working-class socialism which Marxism had named in its most basic doctrine — advanced capitalist society and economy. The Russian state set itself up by overthrowing the working class regime established in 1917. The other Stalinist regimes developed through agencies very different from the politically-aware working class to which Marxists looked as agency; and without the democracy which Marxists saw as an essential political precondition for collective ownership by society. They were political formations whose ideas and typical actions had been rejected and denounced in advance by Marxists, Bolsheviks, socialists. It is a frame-up!

B. No! It tags you fair and square for what you are.

A. If you insist, use words like socialism and communism to describe the horrors of the 20th century, and choose another name for what I'm calling socialism — "democratic collectivism", or a less clumsy term, if you can think of one. Maybe "consistent democrats" best covers it. But stop fooling yourself with the pretence that Stalinism and its like were what Marx and Lenin talked about and acted for. Or what they defined as scientific socialism. Stop blinding yourself! Stop misleading those who take your misrepresentations as intellectual good coin. Stop brandishing Stalinism as a scarecrow against those who fought Stalinism and, of course, fascism, to the death. Stop using the old horrors of Stalinism to excuse the present horrors of capitalism. Stop pretending that the fundamental and explosive contradictions generated by the very development of capitalism have gone away, or that they will go away of their own accord.

B. Suicide is not a solution to the problems that go with being alive. Suicide-by-socialism is not a solution to the social and economic problems of life under capitalism.

The only possible economic basis for social liberty is market capitalism. "Liberticide" is too self-murdering and others-murdering a price for eliminating the faults and difficulties of capitalism.

Whatever the difficulties, under capitalism we have democracy, liberty, the right to life and to pursue individual happiness.

A. What you and others like you do is a form of ideological bully-work, or intellectual terrorism, in the first place against yourselves. Stop frightening yourself into know-nothing mindlessness. Stop blinding yourself with a-historical and radically false accounts of capitalism and Stalinism, both! Stop comforting yourself with old Stalinist lies! Your approach has inhibited god knows how many people of good will from drawing the logical socialist conclusions from the crisis of world capitalism since 2007-8. Socialism? they think. No, that is that old Stalinist horror story we all know so well. Stop using Stalinism as the great scarecrow of history to frighten away all serious discussion of capitalism and its place in history, as well as of socialism. Stop pretending that liberty and the right to pursue happiness are tied to capitalist exploitation and de facto plutocratic rule, and inseparable from it. And, if you want it in a nutshell: Stalinism did not kill socialism because it did not kill capitalism, whose achievements and whose defects have generated and will generate socialist working-class anti-capitalism.

The Russian Revolution, Socialism, and Democracy

B. You try to separate your socialism from the historical record of Stalinism. For credibility you need to. And your better model for both socialism and democracy is what — the "Trotskyist tradition"? The feeble Bolshevik anti-Stalinist tradition? Like the good intentions of Lenin and Trotsky, and poor old Rosa Luxemburg, that counts for nothing. It is the Cheshire Cat's hologram-smile after it has vanished and been replaced by a rabid, snarling wild beast. Their good intentions are confined to the margins of the story! Your retrospective good intentions count for even less, far less. For nothing but self-bamboozlement.

A. It is plain fact that the system that got locked into place at the end of the civil war, at the 10th congress of the Bolshevik party in March 1921, and the controlled unleashing then of market forces, paved the way to Stalinism. It could even be argued that, with their forced collectivisation and breakneck command-industrialisation after 1928, the Stalinists, or some of them, may have drawn some of their inspiration and models from the "war communism" of the civil war period. And, yes, by, let us say, 1930, Stalinism was a full-fledged, though not yet stabilised, totalitarian system

B. Being Bolsheviks, the civil-war leaders cleared the way for Stalinism!

A. The banning of factions in the party in 1921 was a tremendous Bolshevik mistake, even though it was intended to be a temporary emergency measure, and assumed that different "platforms" could still operate in the party.

B. Bolshevism was its own first mistake!

A. Bolshevism was much more than its mistakes. One of the first things the Bolsheviks did in power was abolish the death penalty! And on 8 November 1917, the day after the Bolshevik-led soviets seized power, with Europe drowning in blood and the world war set to go on for another year, they issued an appeal for immediate peace, an end to the war on the basis of freedom and self-determination for all nations and peoples.

B. Appeals are cheap — cheap as paper! Cheap as the airwaves to broadcast such things!

A. A pity the other belligerent parties didn't respond with their own "cheap" appeals for peace, but went on with the slaughtering. In just two of the biggest battles of the war between the time of the Bolsheviks' appeal and the eventual armistice of 11 November 1918, no fewer than 804,100 men were killed and wounded in the second battle of the Somme, and 319,200 killed and wounded in the second battle of the Marne. About 160,000 soldiers were killed in those two battles.

B. At least the other governments were honest — unlike the Bolsheviks.

A. Honest imperialist butchers? No, not even that: they said they fought the war "to end war", and for the self-determination of small nations.

Listen: "The workers' and peasants' government... calls upon all the belligerent peoples and their government to start immediate negotiations for a just, democratic peace. By a just or democratic peace... the government means an immediate peace without annexations (i.e., without the seizure of foreign lands, without the forcible incorporation of nations in states alien to them) and without indemnities...

"The government proposes an immediate armistice to the governments and people of all the belligerent countries, and, for its part, considers it desirable that this armistice should be concluded for a period of not less than three months, i.e., a period long enough to permit the completion of negotiations for peace..."

B. They didn't stick to that peaceful approach, though, did they? Therefore, it was not for them a code they lived by — it was hypocrisy.

A. They could not, in a fierce civil war and in face of invading foreign armies, confine themselves to good pacifist rules for living in a future world not yet realised. They had to fight for that future against the ruling-class gangs that had been stifling Europe and Russia in blood since 1914.

B. Don't you see the irony, the absurdity, in what you have just said?

A. To refuse to use force and violence in the struggle would be to let their own side be overwhelmed by the force, violence and homicide of their enemies. They lived and fought in a pre-socialist world, a world plunged death-deep into neo-barbarism, in order to act upon it and change it for the better. The Bolsheviks did not make a lifestyle out of their aspirations: they made their aspirations the inspiration for a determined battle in their here-and-now to realise their aspirations.

B. So their ideals were meaningless! And by dropping out of the war, they strengthened German militarism against the Allies.

THE RUSSIAN REVOLUTION, SOCIALISM, AND DEMOCRACY

A. Their ideals gripped the minds of workers and soldiers in the warring countries and especially in Germany, where there was a great socialist tradition. They helped foment the German revolution which brought down the Kaiser in October-November 1918 and brought the great capitalist slaughter to an end.

B. They just did whatever would help them keep the power they had grabbed.

A. Someone, arguing that Bolshevik and Stalinist were the same because the Bolsheviks, too, used violence, once said that in this the Bolsheviks had the morality of "Kaffirs". Trotsky responded: "First of all such a contemptuous reference to the Kaffirs is hardly proper from the pen of 'socialists'... If we should tell the toiler-Kaffir how the workers arose in a part of our planet and caught their exploiters unawares, he would be very pleased".

B. The Bolsheviks built an authoritarian state! That is the verdict of history on Lenin and Trotsky.

A. Yes, but *whose* history? Whose verdict is that?

B. The verdict of all decent people who know the facts.

A. Of prejudiced and devoutly ignorant people like you, stifled in self-mind-numbing animosity. The Bolsheviks, knowing they had a majority in the great congress of Soviets due to start on 25 October (on the old calendar; 7 November on the new), seized power on 24-25 October. On 25-26 October the Congress of Soviets, the most democratic parliament in Russian or any other history, endorsed the Bolshevik uprising and set up a new government.

B. The Bolsheviks made a coup d'état. The idea that there was a working-class revolution is only a myth to comfort people like you. It was a Bolshevik coup; a seizure of power by the incipient totalitarians.

A. It was a seizure of power from an unelected government, which had minority support, and dwindling support at that, by people who led the majority in the most democratic parliament in history, a workers' and farmers' parliament — the Soviet. That was a revolution, not a coup. It licensed and triggered a great revolution made by the workers and peasants all through Russian society. Do you know that in 1918, the workers seized the factories and drove out the employers, ignoring the plea of the government, which wanted to move much more slowly? Coup, indeed!

B. So what? Working-class action is not self-sanctifying! To call it the most democratic parliament anywhere, more democratic than Britain, the USA, or France, is ridiculous!

A. US democracy even today is shackled by entrenched plutocratic rule and 18th century Whig "safeguards" and restraints against too precipitate democracy. The unelected Supreme Court has as much and maybe more power than Congress! In all the countries you list, in 1917 the vote was restricted. Women lacked the right to vote in all of them, with the exception of votes for state affairs in some recently-frontier states of the USA. French and Belgian women did not get the right to vote until 1945. In Switzerland, believe it or not, women got the right to vote as late as 1971. In Britain large sections of the men of the working class could not vote until 1918 because they did not meet property qualifications. Women over 30 got the vote in 1918. They didn't get the vote on the same terms as those men got in 1918, at the age of 21, until a decade later.

The elections in the Soviets had no constraints of property or gender. The Soviet Congress could not be vetoed by an appointed-not-elected Supreme Court. Nowhere else did the electorate have the right to recall their deputies at will, and elect new ones. The Congress of Soviets which met on 25 October (7 November) 1917 and appointed a government was indeed the most democratic parliament in history. The Bolshevik and Left-SR government it appointed was, therefore, the most democratic government in history.

B. They overthrow the previous government in a coup!

A. If the Bolsheviks had not overthrown the unelected Kerensky government, then it would probably soon have been overthrown by some would-be military dictator. An attempted military coup, by General Kornilov, had been defeated in August 1917. It was in defeating that coup that the Bolsheviks gained a great deal of the political strength that they used in October.

B. It was the Bolsheviks, not the working class, that took power.

A. Representative bodies of the working class and the peasants took power and elected a government. Bolshevik-led workers backed by the peasants, and the workers' and peasants' Congress of Soviets, their parliament, took power. It is possible to argue, as anarchists do, that "representative government" is a contradiction in terms, and that the individuals who "hold power" are always just individuals, just themselves, and that the working class as such cannot hold power, ever. But that is an argument against representative government in general. Apply it to Britain today!

B. Not a class, but a whole nation, stands behind British governments!

A. No. A majority of elected MPs stands behind British governments, but that is all. Up until the Falklands war of 1982, the Thatcher government that wrought such changes in British society, that presided from mid-1979 over the destruction of much of the old industries, that imposed legal shackles on trade unionists, that banned solidarity strikes, that condemned a generation of working-class youth to the social scrapheap — that government had only minority support according to the opinion polls of the time. In 1980-1 Labour led the Tories in the polls by usually around 10%, often around 15 or even 20%.

B. But it was the elected government!

A. No matter who had voted for it, and even if most workers had voted for it (they didn't), the Thatcher government functioned as a government of the capitalist class, an especially vicious one. So too did the Tory/ Lib-Dem government after 2010. Socialists thought — and argued at the time — that working-class direct action to resist the Thatcher government was democratically legitimate, and, indeed, a healthy part of a functioning democracy, no matter how big a majority in Parliament Thatcher had.

B. Those socialists were not democrats!

A. In fact, we were. The weekly paper *Socialist Organiser* campaigned for an extension of existing democracy. But we recognised the social and political realities of the time. Irreversible social and economic damage was being inflicted on the working class and on British society as a whole. As it happened, that was done without a specific electoral sanction. But, irrespective of that, the victims had a right to resist a tyrannous government of the capitalist class. Even the American constitution asserts and upholds the right of revolt against a tyrannical government.

B. That sort of direct action is against democracy! The leader of the Labour Party, Michael Foot, said so at the time.

A. That's what he shouted at the left as he surrendered to the class-war Tory government. He was wrong even on democracy. People of your political persuasion will resort, and have resorted, to "direct action" to resist working-class or left-wing governments that "interfere with" the capitalist system. Michael Foot simply threw in the towel. In fact, one of his urgent motives was fear of a British military coup like the coup that had erupted in Chile in September 1973 against a moderately left-wing elected government.

B. The Bolsheviks dispersed the real democratic parliament in Russia! In January 1918 they closed down the elected Constituent Assembly.

A. Yes, they dispersed the Constituent Assembly. But the idea that the Constituent Assembly was more democratic than the Soviets, with their right to recall and to replace their delegates at any time — that's preposterous. And ignorant. The Constituent Assembly was elected on lists of candidates finalised before the Soviet Congress of October-November 1917. The biggest bloc of elected deputies was that of the "Socialist Revolutionary" party, but in October the "Socialist Revolutionaries" had split into "Left SRs", who in November formed a coalition government with the Bolsheviks, and "Right SRs", who walked out of the Congress of Soviets. If they'd had the strength, the "Right SRs" would have dispersed the Congress of Soviets as the Soviets dispersed the Constituent Assembly. The "Left SRs", who were the majority of the old SR party, were under-represented on the Constituent Assembly lists drawn up before their party split, and the "Right SRs" over-represented.

B. They should not have dismissed the elected parliament.

A. Even if one agrees with Rosa Luxemburg, an ardent supporter of the Bolsheviks, that it would have been better for the Soviet majority not to dismiss the Constituent Assembly — and I'm not saying that I do — democracy is not the issue. It was the democracy of the Soviets, led politically by the Bolsheviks, initially in coalition with the Left SRs, against the democracy of the Constituent Assembly, led by the Right SRs. When the English bourgeoisie was fighting Stuart absolutism, to make a beginning of parliamentary rule, Oliver Cromwell too dismissed a Parliament.

B. The Constituent Assembly was more representative. All classes, not just the workers and peasants, were represented in it.

A. And that would have given it the right to override the Soviet majority, which certainly represented the majority of the people, peasants and workers alike? The point was that the working class and most of the peasants were in the process of overthrowing the bourgeoisie and the landlords and their rule. The exigencies of class struggle were decisive, not the notion that everybody's vote was equal to everyone else's. Your idea of what is democratic and anti-democratic defines itself here, and plainly, as a conception of limited democracy. Your democracy means the right of the ruling class and their supporters to override even a democratic majority. (A bit like the US Constitution, in fact.) Here you call the necessary action of the representatives of that majority, when they act as the majority, a coup!

B. The Constituent Assembly was the supreme Parliament. It had the duty, as well as the right, to oppose the Soviet pretend-parliament!

A. Who but the people, the workers and farmers, could say which was the real and which the pretend parliament? They backed the soviet

Government, which legislated in favour of what they were already doing on the land and in the factories. The limited democracy you advocate is, as I've already said, bourgeois democracy, plutocratic democracy. The idea of economic, social, democracy does not even occur to you. Your "democratic" face is set against it.

B. I am against the robbery of one class by another under the flag of democracy, or any other flag.

A. Are you? In fact, no, you're not! You side with the landlord and capitalist robbers of the people. In Russia then, and in Britain now. Essentially, your position is that representative democracy, the election of deputies, is no real democracy. But only for the Russian revolutionaries. For Britain, France, the USA, etc., you raise no objection to it. Against the working-class regime set up in 1917 you postulate — by implication, I mean — some undefined super-democracy, and counterpose it as an ideal to the real, historically-evolved, Soviet democracy.

The story of the 1984-5 miners' strike, which shook the Tory government and would have won if labour movement leaders had come good on their promises of support, is told in a book from Workers' Liberty.

www.workersliberty.org/books

Spanish dockworkers march in a dispute over jobs, early 2017. Indian women home workers march in protest. 84% of India's workforce is "informal" — that is, hyper-casual — and 18% of urban workers pursue their trades at home. Yet even the home workers are organising.

Part 5: Democracy and socialism

Is democracy central to socialism?

B. I say that your socialist ranting will never achieve anything positive. All such wild talk may do is undermine the real democracy we have now. Socialists simply do not understand or appreciate democracy.

A. Codswallop! For socialists — serious socialists, Marxian socialists — democracy is a central, all-conditioning and all-defining, principle and central value of our socialism. Without democracy, genuinely socialist collective ownership is impossible. The socialist criticism of parliamentary democracy is not an opposition to democracy or a rejection of it. We want a better democracy. We say that the pluto-democracy, money-bourgeois-democracy we have now, under capitalism, is the shallowest, emptiest version of democracy.

B. It's a damn sight better than any form of authoritarianism or absolutism or totalitarianism!

A. Yes it is! I don't want to deny that. Our different ideas about the necessary economic basis for liberty and democracy are what divides us here. Of course we are for liberty and democracy! The socialist who is not for democratic self-rule and liberty in relation to the state and society is not a socialist but a walking contradiction in terms. And the other way round, too. The anti-socialist who is against extending democracy to the economic conditions in which people's lives have to be lived is not really a democrat.

B. You want to tear down the real democracy we have in the name of unrealistic dreams of some ideal future democracy!

A. What strikes me most is how unambitious you and your sort are for the democracy and liberty you claim as your guiding principles, your political lodestone. For a start you praise what we call bourgeois democracy for such things as liberty. These are distinct and separable things. Unenlightened democracy can be the enemy of liberty. You conflate democracy and liberty. Thereby you obscure the relationship between them and block discussion of the most important questions: democracy, yes, but how and for whom? Liberty — whose liberty? You settle for a miserably reduced, diminished, docked, stulted, dwarf, and often mere token version of the liberty and democracy you glorify. We have a deeper, older, and more comprehensive idea of democracy. We are more ambitious for democracy.

B. Older?

A. The common meanings of both democracy and liberty today are emaciated, ruinously diminished, versions of the ideas put forward 100, 150, 200 or more years ago by the pioneer fighters for liberty and democracy. The Jacobin zealots of the great French revolution, like Maximilien Robespierre and Louis Antoine de Saint-Just, or even the radical leaders of the American Revolution, such as Thomas Jefferson, or the mid-19th century Chartist labour-movement champions of democracy and liberty in Britain, or the leaders of the 1916 Rising in Dublin — Connolly, Pearse, and all the others who fought for liberty and democracy — none of them would recognise our version of liberty and democracy as the realisation and embodiment of what they advocated under the same names. They would see it for what it is. Maximum freedom for the rich to do what they like to the poor throughout the world! None of them would accept as theirs what you in your fear-ridden Stalinophobic funk champion and defend as democracy! They would call it a fraud.

B. Yes, socialists don't defend real liberty and democracy. You, now, for instance: you disparage and undermine it.

A. Some would-be socialists don't champion liberty and democracy. Serious socialists, consistently Marxist socialists, do. And we have for many decades. Trotsky did.

B. Socialists are usually in the vanguard — to use your jargon — of every "politically correct" attempt to control, regulate, stifle and suppress the free expression of ideas. Not just the horrible and insulting n-word and things like that...

A. Even the most repressive, or the silliest, of the "politically correct" zealots as a rule starts out with legitimate concern about real injustice against black people, women, gay people, physically or mentally disabled people...

You accept that the n-word, which encapsulates petrified age-old prejudice, and the memory of the enslavement of black people, should be suppressed. Yes, "politically correct" people are sometimes superstitious, authoritarian, repressive, regressive even. They sometimes make rational discussion difficult or even impossible. They try to banish real injustices and bad attitudes by bits of what might be called "verbal engineering". That should be opposed. But get your priorities right!

B. And your priorities?

IS DEMOCRACY CENTRAL TO SOCIALISM?

A. For 30 years now, in Britain, privatisation has been very unpopular. A poll in 2013 found majorities for public ownership of 68% (energy companies), 67% (Royal Mail), 66% (rail), and 84% (NHS), with only small minorities positively for privatisation.

Yet for those same 30 years, government after government has continued to privatise. That happens because there is great pressure, through a million channels, on the larger parties that might oppose privatisation, like the Labour Party, to hew to big-business interests on issues which big business considers important. Because it is very difficult for new parties to make their way unless they have substantial backing in the moneyed classes. Because there is little scope for the electorate to influence a government once it takes office. It settles in to work with the permanent unelected state hierarchy, and with the big, rich, entrenched, "vested interests". It is immersed in the flows of big-business lobbying. The Blair Labour government came to office with a very popular promise to reverse the Tories' marketisation of the Health Service. Then it pushed the marketisation much further than the Tories had done; and the voters had no redress.

We have a very deficient, inadequate form of democracy. The truth is that, in the very broad historical sense in which the Liberals can claim to be of the left, the left has failed and failed first and last as democrats — that is, failed to secure a system that functions democratically in Abraham Lincoln's apt definition: "government of the people, by the people, for the people". Today's pluto-democracy is government of the rich, by the rich, for the rich, and a few sops sometimes for the people.

B. You're so f'ing negative! You are a destructive utopian idiot!

A. Well, I do the best I can! The question posed on democracy in historical experience is this: what is the economic basis needed for democracy to exist in reality as well as in name — democracy all through the economy and society as well as in politics — what the early democrats advocated.

Today's democracy means a society in which the means of production, exchange, and communication are monopolised by a small class of vastly rich people, and administered for their benefit, not that of society or of the workers. Economic decisions of vast importance are taken by that small class — look at the bankers, for god's sake! That system cannot honestly be called democratic. Saying that it is preferable to outright dictatorship — which is true — doesn't settle the question, or get you off the hook.

B. You are the one who is on the hook!

A. In such a system democratic political structures cannot but be a facade for the autocrats who own industry and make the fundamental social decisions that shape the lives of all of us.. The government, in the fundamental things, is their "executive committee". I repeat: this "plutodemocracy" is not what the great pioneer fighters for democracy and liberty would recognise as democracy if they could come and look at it and had to live in it.

B. History evolves, ideas are tempered and modified in experience. That's unavoidable. Usually it's good.

Dhaka, Bangladesh, 2013: workers demonstrate for safety at work after the collapse of the Rana Plaza building, which housed many factories producing garments for global markets on sub-contracts to well-known brands, killed 1127 workers.

The Evolution of Democracy

A. In the long-ago days of small enterprises and farm homesteads, in late 18th century America, democrats could in principle assume a society of more or less equal citizens who would vote, and whose votes had a roughly equal weight. In our world, all in theory are equal, but some, in George Orwell's words satirising Stalinism, "are more equal than others". A lot more! In Britain today, just one thousand of the wealthiest people have between them more wealth than the poorest 40% of households. In the USA, the top 0.1% own as much household wealth as the lower 90%. Think of those astonishing figures!

And the wealthy have more "liberty", too. When the freedom of the press in practice means freedom for newspaper and other media owners like Rupert Murdoch, Richard Desmond, or Berlusconi, that is liberty not of the people but liberty against the people — the companion to a democracy that is a withered, mocking parody of real and full democratic self-rule.

B. There are shortcomings. Maybe some of them can be remedied, maybe most of them are inevitable limitations which arise from living in a complex, intractable society. In any case, actually existing democracy with its shortcomings is vastly better than the total suppression of democracy which you had under socialism.

A. Under Stalinism! What you say here is the proof that if we let the memory of the Stalinist horrors that went under variants of the name "socialism" inhibit us in drawing the necessary conclusions from our own situation and about what capitalism now is and must be, then in the here and now we disarm, ideologically and politically. We paralyse ourselves. The demonisation of "socialism", the insistence that the murdering Stalinist liars were correct when they presented their system as socialism, is a central part of the bourgeoisie's "class struggle on the ideological front", the "battle of ideas", now. It functions to prevent people thinking and drawing the logical democratic as well as socialist conclusions from Stalinism then and capitalism now.

B. It's still a case of "they're all out of step except me and my comrade, Johnny"! You are trying to "deny", deconstruct, talk away the great fact that there is such a thing in our world as real democracy. It is real, whatever its limits, and however much you say it might be improved upon.

A. I probe and evaluate things democratic as part of advocating improved, or qualitatively better, democracy. Do you think that the existing forms of bourgeois democracy need no criticism and debunking? That there is no need for improvement or transformation? You insist on identifying criticism of "actually existing" democracy with hostility to democracy. Thereby you erect insurmountable barriers against critical examination and judgement.

B. Your destructive criticism promotes an authoritarian socialist agenda!

A. You are like the poor silly guy in the old satire who, confronted with earthquakes, fires, and other catastrophes, insisted: "All is for the best in the best of all possible worlds". You are saying that existing democracy is the best of all possible democracies, and existing society the best of all possible societies. You are also saying: please don't criticise democracy too roughly, lest it fall apart. Is it that fragile?

B. No, but I say: leave well enough alone.

A. As between the rich and the poor, bourgeois, plutocratic, "actually existing" democracy is not a "level playing field". It is a great deal less than democratic in all the most important ways. The rich have immense advantages. Think of the repulsive and fascist-minded ignoramus Donald Trump winning the 2016 US presidential election! He could do that because he is rich. The great corporations and people like Trump have and use immense political weight in shaping public policy. The individual citizen is feeble in comparison, and on most things has no possibility of competing with them. The rich can spend tens of millions putting their candidates of choice into the House of Representatives and the Senate, and, usually, the Presidency — that is, buying them in advance by financing them, tying them by pre-election political "mortgages" on their future conduct.

And then they fund, to the tune of about $9 billion a year, a political lobbying industry which is estimated to employ 100,000 people in all its offshoots. Take averages, and each of the 500-odd members of Congress has an average of 200 lobby-industry people on her or his case. An average of $18 million a year is spent on lobbying each member of Congress.

B. That's only the USA.

A. Not only the USA, by any means. A book published in 2014 estimated the lobbying industry in Britain at £2 billion a year, which is an average of £3 million a year per individual MP. And lobbying comes from the unelected supremos of the permanent state machine as well as from designated lobbyists. In his book about the experience of the Labour government from 1964 to 1970, Harold Wilson described how Lord Cromer, the Governor of the Bank of England, insisted on social cuts as soon as Labour came to office. "I asked him [Cromer, governor of the Bank of England] if this meant that it was impossible for any government, whatever its party label, whatever its manifesto or the policies on which it fought an election, to continue, unless it immediately reverted to full-scale Tory policies... We had now reached the situation where a newly elected government was being told by international speculators that the policy on which we had fought the election could not be implemented: that the government was to be forced into adoption of Tory policies to which it was fundamentally opposed... The Queen's First Minister was being asked to bring down the curtain on parliamentary democracy by accepting the doctrine that an election in Britain was a farce, that the British people could not make a choice between policies". But prime minister Wilson nevertheless did what Cromer asked. The number of people who see no point in bothering to vote in national elections testifies to their awareness of the limits of this democracy, even if their mood is often no more than a general feeling that politics is irrelevant, and all politicians are people on the make.

B. Obama proved the opposite.

A. Obama's election proved that the "little citizen" can sometimes assert herself against the corporate "Big Citizens". But look what happened when Obama tried to change things — the weight the pharmaceutical industry and the private health-insurance sellers thrown against proper social medicine; the political clout the gun industry and its National Rifle Association deploy in preventing painfully necessary limits to the availability of guns, and so on.

Remember that it was known for decades that smoking caused cancer, and that the information was obscured, diluted, and denied by the tobacco industry and on its behalf. It was decades before social regulation began.

B. That's democracy! That's pluralism.

A. No, that's "plute-democracy"! Tremendous economic powers and social-financial forces dominate the democratic discourse, the elections, the shaping of opinion and public policy. And they buy the legislators.

B. It's the best we've got. Your criticisms can only erode respect for it. Then we may get worse.

A. Don't raise a rude dissenting voice in church, eh? Mere individual citizens or associations of citizens ordinarily have no chance of competing with the corporate "Big Citizens" and rich individual citizens. That's the truth.

B. You'd prefer it if all the "Big Citizens" confronted the "little citizens" as one giant state corporation, as one corporate "Big Brother Citizen"?

A. I'd prefer it if society ran what the "Big Citizens" now run in the interests of all instead of, as now, letting it be run in the private interests of the "Big Citizens". I'd prefer it if democracy were not a thing of politics only, if the power of the multiple-vote-possessing Big Citizens were taken from them.

B. They don't have more than one vote!

A. Through influence and wealth they dispose of many votes! If democracy meant economic democracy, for the most important instance, then people could democratically control the conditions that shape their lives locally, nationally, and beyond the individual nations. Now, we can't do that or anything like it.

B. That's double-talk.

A. The wretched system you champion subsists on "double-talk"! For example, capitalist vested interests do their best to hide the facts about global warming. They have falsified the records and set up tame scientists, that is, bought-and-paid-for prostitute experts, to hinder the flow of real knowledge and real discussion. They have warped, diluted, and smothered serious discussion. To cliché it, they poison the wells of the public information which is irreplaceable for real democratic opinion-formation and decision-making. The social realities of capitalist class rule determine most of the time what really-existing democracy is in practice.

B. Yes, but democracy prevails.

A. No, it doesn't!

B. Not always and immediately. But in the long run democracy will prevail.

A. God is good, eh? Hope and pray! Normally, usually, it takes tens of millions of dollars to run for any high national office in the USA.

B. People can club together small sums and pool money to back a candidate.

A. What kind of democracy is it with such enormous tariff walls against poorer people standing in elections? It is worse than the old system in Britain, before 1911, of not paying MPs, and thereby ensuring that only well-off people could be MPs. Normally less than half the US electorate votes.

B. People paid by private associations could be MPs. Trade unions and the early Labour Party financed their own MPs before 1911, people like Keir Hardie. And the point is, surely, that people in the USA have the choice of voting or not voting.

A. The point about so many, even of the registered voters, usually not bothering to vote is that so few people believe that their vote gives them a real voice in what's happening. And in the UK there are about seven million eligible people, about 13% of those eligible, not even registered to vote.

B. Nothing is perfect! I don't say it's perfect, only that it is better than any known alternative.

A. Not so. History has known a better democratic alternative — soviets, the democracy of workers' councils, a real representative democracy. For sure, nothing in existing democracy — bourgeois democratic, plutocratic democracy — is perfect. It is not even adequate. Consider: everyone knows fictions like Anthony Hope's *The Prisoner of Zenda*, or Mark Twain's *The Prince and The Pauper*, in which in some "Ruritania" or Tudor England without democracy a commoner who looks like one of the rulers takes his place for a while. A decade or so ago, I saw an American "Ruritanian" equivalent of Twain and Hope, *Dave*, set in the USA in our times. Dave, a goodhearted, benign, socially responsible man, owns a small-town employment agency, and he happens to look like the President. A stroke makes the President a vegetable, and conniving politicians substitute Dave for him.

Dave, the good guy, sponsors all sorts of New-Deal-style Rooseveltian schemes to help the needy and uses his borrowed power to push them through the clogged-up democratic (or, so often in reality, pretendedly democratic) system.

B. Ah, you tell fairy stories: light relief from socialist gobbledegook! Go on.

A. The film was far from being the biting satire it might have been, but think about what its production tells you about American democracy now. A lot of people feel so excluded that there is a market for an American-Ruritanian romance.

B. There have been lots of films like that, for example Frank Capra's *Mr Smith Goes To Washington*.

A. No, those were about citizens intervening into the "political process". Dave was about a good-king president bypassing or subverting the system, borrowing the king-president's power in order to do good with it that the real president would never have done.

B. OK, it is not perfect. It is the best we've got. You know what Churchill, I think it was, said? The best argument for democracy is the alternatives. And of course it's secure! It's the future.

A. The enormous number of people normally not voting; the plutocratic costs of standing for office in the USA; the fact that a "free press" means freedom of billionaires to monopolise the means of forming public opinion — these facts and more signal a serious atrophy in existing bourgeois democracy.

B. And what about the new social media?

A. That makes a difference, a big difference perhaps. It was a factor in Obama being able to stand for president, and Sanders being able to run for the Democratic nomination in 2016. But that only modifies the main picture. The plain truth is that social evolution, the emergence over the last 150-200 years of economic "Giant Citizens", has rendered obsolete and inadequate the old forms of a democracy designed for a radically different age and society. Essentially it is the same social process that happened when economic-exploitative giants grow up inside the small-owner economy that went with the old democracy.

B. Nobody says there isn't room for improvement.

A. But that's just waffle and evasion. I say we urgently need radical "improvement". We need something qualitatively different. You know what your big trouble here is? I'll say it again. You are far too unambitious in your democratic aspirations. You are hag-ridden with historical funk. Ridiculously, suicidally unambitious! You boast of "democracy", yet there is a glaring, obvious, timidity and uncertainty about it for you. Isn't there?

B. Timidity? No, I'm just sticking to something real, in place of wild promises of something better when in fact, in history, such promises often led to something worse. A parliamentary democracy of all the people is better than a class-limited Soviet democracy (as you call it). By definition it is more democratic.

A. The truth is that such all-in democracy hides and disguises the rule of the bourgeoisie, and, in its pretensions to be an all-inclusive democracy, it functions mainly to evoke consent for bourgeois governments, or the pretence of such consent.

B. It is real consent.

A. Yes, manufactured consent, consent which is in large part a resigned acceptance of what the entrenched power structures make to seem inevitable. The Soviets of 1917 assumed the right to ride roughshod over the bourgeoisie and the landlords and what had seemed inevitable under their rule. That, by the way, is what the Bolsheviks understood by "dictatorship of the proletariat". They did not think of it as a single person's dictatorship, or as what the Stalinists created, but as the rule of a class, organised democratically and acting "dictatorially" to override entrenched ruling-class laws, traditions, and state institutions.

B. Again: you are against parliamentary democracy!

A. No, I'm not against parliamentary democracy! Not if the alternative is some sort of authoritarian or totalitarian political system. In 1934 Trotsky and his comrades advocated that the French working class defend parliamentary democracy, then under threat by fascists: "As long as the majority of the working class continues on the basis of bourgeois democracy, we are ready to defend it with all our forces against violent attacks from the Bonapartist and fascist bourgeoisie". At the time he put forward a program to improve that democracy, and we have the same approach today. "A single assembly must combine the legislative and executive powers. Members would be elected for two years, by universal suffrage at eighteen years of age, with no discrimination of sex or nationality. Deputies would be elected on the basis of local assemblies, constantly revocable by their constituents, and would receive the salary of a skilled worker. This is the only measure that would lead the masses forward instead of pushing them backward. A more generous democracy would facilitate the struggle for workers' power". That was and is our attitude to parliamentary democracy.

B. Trotsky was being hypocritical!

A. No, he wasn't. Why should he be? He meant exactly what he wrote. So did the French Trotskyists who advocated those things in a crisis of parliamentary democracy, when fascists surrounded the Parliament (and the French Communist Party also called for people to join the street demonstration).

B. Trotsky was hypocritical if he said that after what the Bolsheviks did to the Constituent Assembly?

A. In France in 1934 there was no alternative parliament, no Congress of Soviets as in Russia in 1917. Yes, we are against bourgeois parliamentary democracy when the alternative is the higher form of democracy embodied in soviets or workers' councils.

B. We? You are royal, or editorial, now, are you?

A. We, the socialists, the movement, the ideas that have continuity from the past to the present and will continue beyond — the tradition. Continuity and tradition are very important things. We can give a precise account of the evolution of our ideas. You can't give a true account of the evolution of your bourgeois ideas on democracy and of the break with earlier conceptions of democracy, in the eyes of its proponents and opponents alike then, which your system now embodies. That is also the answer to your question, why Trotsky? Trotsky was the Spartacus of the 20th century, the leader with Lenin of the working-class revolt, and also the Kepler, the scientist groping for a full and accurate understanding of his contemporary society and history.

B. Yes, groping — in self-induced and self-sustained political, intellectual, and moral darkness.

Vestas factory occupation, 2009: workers occupied what was then Britain's only wind turbine blade factory, in the Isle of Wight, to save "green jobs"

Democracy in British History

A. If democracy doesn't go forward, develop and expand, then it tends to atrophy, hollow out, lose vitality, and it may begin to regress. That is certainly true when democracy lacks living roots in the economic system, as ours does. In Britain, democracy has expanded and improved in stages to take most of the people into the franchise. After the Revolution of 1688, Parliament, not the King, ruled, but it was a parliament on only a very limited franchise. As Marx analysed it, a Whig aristocratic caste ruled for the whole bourgeoisie. In 1832, 144 years after the 1688 Whig revolution, the new middle class was admitted to the vote and electoral boundaries were changed so as to give representation to the new centres of manufacturing such as Manchester and Birmingham. Many of the male urban proletarians were admitted to the vote in 1867, and some of the rural poor in 1884. Property qualifications meant that large swathes of poor males were still without votes. And, of course, no woman, not even a very rich woman, had a vote. In 1918 men who hadn't had the property to qualify under the old system got the vote, and so did women, but not yet on the same basis as men. Men could vote at 21, women only at 30. Women finally got franchise equality with men in 1929.

B. That's just what I need, a rehash of school-kid history.

A. Are you sure you don't?

B. You accept that democracy has progressively improved, don't you? Whatever the shortcomings in the past, it's good now, or anyway, a great deal better.

A. Have you ever come across the idea that the best de facto constitution Britain has had was in the 35 years between the admission of the bourgeoisie to the vote in 1832, and the admission of some of the urban working class in 1867?

B. Now you go on from school-kid history to eccentric glosses on the British constitution!

A. I was startled by the idea that 1832-67 was the ideal system of bourgeois democracy when I first came upon it, long ago, in a book by a serious historian of democracy and other things, W E H Lecky, published at the end of the 19th century.

B. Serious historian? Crank, surely?

A. A serious, much-respected, and in his time very prominent historian. He wrote a multi-volumed history of Britain in the 18th century. He published a big history of Ireland which academics dealing with the period of the 1798 Rising and the United Irishmen are still quoting. Initially a supporter of Irish Home Rule, he ended up a Liberal Unionist MP in 1895-1903. His idea about the British constitution between the first and second Reform Acts was very simple and, I think, true from his point of view. It is a mirror-image of what Marxists say, from our point view, about bourgeois democracy. Before 1867, when some of the urban workers got the vote, there was a more or less tight identity between the electorate and the men of property. Therefore, there could be a responsible self-administering democracy.

B. It wasn't what we call democracy today!

A. From our working-class point of view, control by the property-owners is exactly what we have today for most of the affairs of the country. Only in 1832-67 it was straightforward and transparent.

B. What do you find good in that system?

A. Nothing, though the transparency then was better than the obfuscation now. The important thing to grasp is that there was then a one-to-one transparent relation between economic and political power. That was altered by the electoral reforms after 1867 which admitted some of the "have-nots" into the old democracy of the "haves". In a sense Lecky merely explained and expounded the meaning of an old key idea in the case for democracy: "No taxation without representation". It also meant: no representation without taxation. Or, that politics should belong to those with a stake in the serious property of the country.

The great paradox in pluto-democracy is that political democracy and economic democracy are splintered. Successive expansions of the electorate admitted the "have-nots" to nominal rule over the property-owning "haves". The ownership of the country did not go with the new official political system or fall in line with it. A gap like a pair of scissors opening came into being between notional political power and real economic and social power. That gap was dealt with by the opening of another gap: between notional political power and real political and social power.

In the 1832-67 system, politics could be open and honest and frank, posing real issues before an educated electorate who were legislating for themselves, the property-owners of the country. You could say: legislation of the people of money, for the people of money, by the people of money. After 1867, politics was no longer, could no longer be, that. It was no longer a matter of self-administration by responsible property-holders. From that came the dominance in politics of demagogy, lies, "spinning", and political cloak-work with politicians acting as matadors to baffle the electoral bulls.

After 1867, ownership was divided from notional political power. The democratic Parliament became separated both from the de facto economic power of the owners, and from effective power over the owners and over property. A doubleness of power was created between a new state bureaucracy, tied by many ties to the owners, on one side, and the increasingly more democratic Parliament on the other.

B. There was always what you call "cloak work"!

A. Yes, of course. But now it became a dominant element in the operation of the whole system. For the first two-thirds of the 19th century, the upper classes feared democracy — the democracy of Robespierre and St Just in the French Revolution, or of Thomas Jefferson after the USA achieved independence — seeing it as rule for the people by the people, and necessarily rule in their interests. Just as rule by the rich was rule in their own interests, so too would be rule by the people. That is how those clamouring for the vote saw it too. When, for example, the British Chartists of the 1830s and 40s demanded the vote, they understood the franchise to mean the gaining of political and economic control. The people who would gain the vote would have their bread-and-butter questions taken care of by an administration of their own — just as those who already had the vote did.

B. That was primitive democracy — an impossible democracy if rich and poor were to coexist peacefully.

A. Yes, indeed. That is why in the political crisis of 1848 the British ruling class were willing to have civil war rather than concede what the Chartists demanded. They mobilised masses of special constables, as well as the army, to beat down the Chartists.

B. And what happened?

A. The Chartists retreated, and thereafter, as capitalism surged to new growth and expansion, Chartism went into a severe decline. Decades later the thread was picked up by the early Marxist organisations and the Independent Labour Party and then the Labour Party, and woven into the fabric of a renewed working-class political movement.

B. Well, evidently the Chartists were mature enough to see that democracy is and must be above class rule, and impossible if it's a case of "winner takes all" in the economy and society.

A. The winners do take "all", all the most important things anyway, only now the rules of the game changed. After 1867 the rich kept their economic and social power behind a facade of "pure democracy", that is, of democracy redefined to mean votes for the people but continued rule for the rich by the rich and their agents. The rich held to what they had and increased it. Bourgeois right, bourgeois norms, and bourgeois privileges remained in place, behind the allegedly "pure" democracy. Democracy became pluto-democracy, democracy of the big property-holders and not of the people, not for the people, not by the people.

B. And so you say that the British constitution between the first and second Reform Acts, between 1832 and 1867, was the best democratic constitution?

A. No, I don't say that. Lecky says it. Lecky's point of view is not mine. But it is tremendously illuminating. It is what serious socialists say — from the other side of the class barricades. He said, from his own bourgeois point of view, what Marxist socialists say: that to be real, political democracy has to have a corresponding basis of economic and social democracy. Socialists want to restore the link between democracy, voting and property, to reunite political forms and economic power in the only way they should be reunited, by collective property governed by all-embracing political and social democracy. Without that, political democracy is shallow, hollow, and demagogic, and far less than its heralds say it is. And in times of crisis it becomes unstable. To be real and historically secure, political democracy has to have a consonant social and economic basis. It has to be coupled either with a restricted franchise or with an economy owned collectively — that is, democratically. In Britain after 1867, a state bureaucracy was built to act as a dual steering system behind political democracy and democratically elected governments and to usurp in fact the rights of any elected government the bourgeoisie did not agree with. Tony Benn told of an incident after Labour won a general election. By accident a file of papers was given him which had a note attached: "For the new minister, if he is not Tony Benn".

In 1848 the Chartists backed down before the concentrated force of the ruling class. They did not change their views on what democracy was, what it had to be if it was really to be democracy, and not a quasi-democratic system with a big element in it of deception and bamboozlement of the people.

B. Surely that was good — creative ambivalence and ambiguity? Without it we wouldn't have our existing democracy, "compromise democracy" if you like. When the lower orders threaten property, then society locks down. You get a Mussolini or Hitler or Franco regime.

A. You get naked and unashamed bourgeois rule through fascist or regular army gangsters.

B. Democracy above the conflicts and interests of class is preferable. "Pure democracy", if you like, is the only possible democracy. And the only possible basis for liberty.

A. Liberty so long as the rulers are not seriously challenged or threatened! The only form of democracy compatible with bourgeois property ownership and de facto political rule in society is that "pure" political democracy which shifts decisive day-to-day economic questions outside its normal scope. At best it can provide a loose legal framework for the economy. In the system administered by "pure democracy", the property of the rich is normally secure. The voting rights and other democratic reforms sought by the Chartists are gutted of the social and economic content of democracy as initially conceived by democrats and anti-democrats alike.

B. But democratic governments *should* be free of the crude self-interest of classes.

A. You reckon? You really believe that they are? If that is what you think democracy should be, then you implicitly condemn the existing democracy, which normally, in most respects, most of the time, serves the crude self-interest of the rich.

B. If that's true, and I don't believe it, it will be sorted out in due time.

A. They will find other dodges. For Christ's sake — the government even lets the rich get away with refusing to pay their taxes! A welfare state may emerge out of a compromise between the mass of the people and the property-owners brokered by reform-socialists, as after 1945 with the British Labour government. In great social crises like that in France in 1936, when there was a general strike and the election of a Popular Front government, big concessions may be made to the workers, for a time. For a long time, even. They are taken back at the first chance that the bourgeoisie gets to do it in safety and without crippling social convulsions. The Thatcherite reaction after 1979 is a limited example of that.

B. That's got nothing to do with the principles of democratic self-government and "pure democracy".

A. Don't kid yourself: we don't have "pure democracy". Such a thing is impossible. Your "pure democracy" is one-dimensional democracy. "Pure democracy" — democracy conceived apart from the economic and social rule of the demos, of the people, in their own interest — becomes "pluto-democracy", social and economic and political rule in the interests of the rich and very rich behind a quasi-democratic facade. It becomes the hybrid thing you see today in Britain and, more nakedly, in the USA.

Democratic governments fight class and social wars on behalf of the big property-owners. A generation ago, the Thatcher government fought a ferocious class war against the working people. For a year it waged brutal class war on the most rebellious section of the working class, the coal miners. After it beat the miners, it rampaged through society, against the interests and rights of the working people. The political and social world we live in has been shaped by the victories of the ruling class under Thatcher then. The trade unions are still legally shackled as a result of those victories. Britain has the most restrictive and repressive trade-union laws in western Europe! Effective trade unionism, that is, solidarity action, is illegal still. "Pure democracy" is a mirage, a sham, in essence a lie or an inverted pyramid of lies.

One of the greatest political achievements in the history of the bourgeoisie was this enthronement of "pure democracy", the separation of democracy from the meaning it had up to the mid 19th century and beyond, which was, to use Abraham Lincoln's fine definition, "rule of the people, for the people, by the people".

B. So you dismiss the vote and civil liberties as shams?

A. In the most serious matters, yes. For instance, during the year-long miners' strike of 1984-5, the government directed the police, when expedient and necessary, to ignore the laws in controlling the miners. For police to stop miners on the highways to prevent them going to picket was illegal; the police did it anyway. Thatcher publicly promised that if necessary laws would be altered to make what the police did legal. That was class war.

B. So the vote and civil liberties are worthless?

A. I didn't say that. Limited though they may be, civil liberties and the franchise are precious rights won by the people, and worth fighting to preserve and extend.

B. Now you are being illogical, or hypocritical like Trotsky in 1934.

A. The vote — and civil liberties going back centuries — were won by the "common people" and the women and men of the working class. They are precious even in their diminished or underdeveloped form. They are springboards for further advance and barriers against political and social regression. Self-asserting workers can give them real social content. They should be defended when they are attacked. And extended, deepened, put on a better socio-economic foundation!

B. Defended even if they are attacked by the authoritarian left?

A. By Stalinists? Yes! As I've had to insist with you, Stalinism was not in fact a left-wing movement, despite what you, and people who share your point of view believe and say.

B. So, democracy doesn't live up to romantic rhetoric from the 19th century? Of course it doesn't! That's human nature for you. All politicians lie and present false prospectuses to the electorate, and socialist politicians more than most.

A. Suddenly you turn cynic! You are an example of how political life under the existing system can make even a naive and credulous bourgeois democrat disablingly cynical. It corrupts your capacity to see possible futures — just as it blinds you to the realities around you now. The mystifications of politics are a consequence of the separation of political democracy from social democracy. Politicians in this system can't tell the full social or political truth. Often they can't openly avow what is really being discussed in political debates. Because of the pretend-democracy to which they bow, they can't with candour speak of the bourgeois minority rule in society and economy and the subordination of the rest of society to their needs and interests. This system is, so to speak, the "democracy of the lie". The big lie that within the democratic shell, the bourgeoisie does not rule society, primarily, where there is conflict, in its own interests.

B. You're the cynic! The know-nothing cynic. Democratic politics is better than you think it is.

A. Is it? You get lies, double-talk, self-misrepresentation, demagogy, the noisy clash of parties over personalities and trivia. You get the political cesspool we live in. You can get the de facto disenfranchisement of large parts of the people, when they have no political party to express and defend their interests, as with the British working class from the Blair-Brown coup in 1994 to the Corbyn victory in 2015.

B. The way to find answers to social problems is through our existing real democracy, not through your chimerical future democracy.

A. Don't be so naïve! There was once something in some countries of the global South, Indonesia and others, officially called "guided democracy". Present-day democracies are all, even the best, though to different extents, "guided democracies".

B. Better than your ideal of "guided socialist authoritarianism".

A. That isn't my ideal! Nor is it the logic of my socialism. Nor what socialists propose. Nor what socialists in history were trying to achieve.

B. But you disparage democracy at every turn! You conjure up a stupid day-dream and substitute it for a proper evaluation and appreciation of the great things we have already, now. You destructively counterpose a "should be" and a "might be" to the good that "is" now. The inescapable implication is that some species of authoritarianism is better. That is the only possible alternative to democracy.

A. Try not to be so "authoritarian" and "totalitarian" yourself in your way of arguing. And try not to be an idiot! Criticism of existing democratic systems implies neither a desire to destroy them without having a better alternative, nor support for some sort of authoritarianism. The problem here is that you see "democracy" as an abstract, classless, a-historical democracy — a "pure democracy" that does not in fact exist.

B. Of course democracy exists.

A. Of course different sorts and degrees of democracy exist. But so, again, do all sorts of limitations of specific democracies. Democracy is not something always equal to itself. No existing democracy is equal to even the better self of its own limited ideal.

If you are serious about democracy and about developing democracy, you need to stand back and look at it in historical perspective. There have been various sorts and durations of parliamentary bourgeois democracy. And other sorts of democracy have existed too.

B. What? The old USSR's "democracy"?

A. No. I mean real soviet democracy — the democracy of the workers' councils that emerged in Russia in 1917, and then in Germany and Austria and Hungary. And even in a few places in Ireland between 1919 and 1922, during the Irish revolution.

B. Ah! The island of saints, scholars, sorrows and soviets! Up the Soviet Republic! Don't be perverse! In any case, none of it lasted long.

A. No. But it did tremendous things while it existed.

B. Not as good as the USA's democracy, for example, which you call mere bourgeois democracy.

Democracy in U.S. History

A. Take the USA's democracy, then. Over 200 years old — or, in historical time, a mere 200 years old! — it was designed (as I think I've said) for a population of small and medium farmers and urban producers and slave-plantation owners. It was an elite democracy, as of course the original Athenian democracy of slave-owning men was. There were a lot of exclusions from the franchise: by religion until 1828, by property requirements until 1856, by race until 1869-70, and by gender until 1919-20. There were also many exclusions from civil liberty, for slaves in the first place and also for indentured servants, people who were white semi-slaves for a set time.

There were vast numbers of black slaves, captured in Africa and put to work in America, or, later, when Britain suppressed the international slave trade, after 1807, produced on US slave-breeding farms. Children bred to slavery would never, so long as the slave system existed, have any rights at all. Not even the right to life, or the right not to be worked to death, or beaten to death, under the slave-driver's whip.

The Native Americans had few rights too. Amerindians did not get the right to be US citizens until 1924. The last state laws excluding them from voting were not abolished until 1957.

Even "civilised" Native Americans had no rights. Early in the 19th century, the so-named "five civilised tribes", including the well-known Cherokees, were forcibly removed from the south-east of the United States and set down in "Indian Territory" in Oklahoma.

B. So marauding savages should have had the vote! That would reconcile them! Great for democracy, too! Citizen Indian, aim your arrow, bullet, knife, or tomahawk not at a settler's head but at the slit in that little ballot box over there!

A. You think bonehead prejudice is funny? Don't be so superior! In some ways, they were morally better than you and yours. Sitting Bull...

B. No! I know already! I've seen the film! He was the political-religious leader of the Lakota Sioux when they destroyed Custer's cavalry — I suppose you'd say "marauding cavalry" — at the battle of Little Big Horn, in 1876. Wiped them out.

A. Yes. Strange though it is, Sitting Bull later joined Buffalo Bill Cody's Wild West show, touring American cities, which he thus saw for the first time. His friend Annie Oakley, the renowned sharp-shooter of the show, recorded his reactions. He was appalled at the raw poverty, the starvation and semi-starvation and homelessness, which he saw in the big cities. He couldn't understand how a system could exist in which children and others died, neglected and starved, while some had stored up riches and lived in extravagant wealth. Amongst his people, such a thing would be impossible. They would share out the food and shelter and whatever they had. Oakley reported that this "savage" gave much of the money he earned from Cody's roadshow to begging children and others.

B. Another unexpected socialist! He'd have joined the Corbyn Labour Party, you think? He would have been a *Guardian* reader, at least. Shame the old bastard was shot eventually.

A. When that "savage" visited the big cities, he journeyed from the simple human society of his people and jumped, so to speak, across the intervening phases of human social history — ancient slavery, serfdom, early capitalism, etc. — to look at their results, the advanced commercial capitalist civilisation that was crowding his people to death and near-annihilation. He was horrified.

B. Of course he couldn't understand! He probably reckoned wealth in the dried scalps of white men and children, and women. Common ownership of the scalps and wigwams?

A. The point is that he saw things fresh, from outside and across millennia of historical time, with uncalloused mind and raw human sensibilities, with a conscience that hadn't been numbed by familiarity, by regular and daily encounters with the horrors of class society. Unlike you, and I'm sorry to say, me as well, too often and in too many ways.

B. US society was being formed, absorbing vast numbers of immigrants. "Give me your poor, your huddled masses..." What do you want to do — roll back the spool of history and give America back to the Amerindians? Would that also mean undoing the effects of America's interaction with the rest of the world, rolling back the last 500 years of world history?

A. No. That isn't possible.

B. It is desirable?

A. Not desirable, either. Talking about it is pointless. It simply isn't possible.

B. Your attitude is reactionary romanticism! The exclusion of Native Americans from the emerging American society and civilisation was not only something done to them. They were self-excluding, because they were in the grip of an all-shaping cultural inertia and conservatism. Tribes fought to maintain their way of life. Do you think that the great plains and prairies should have been left to a handful of Native Americans as hunting grounds? That we should give the USA and Canada back to them?

A. "We"?

B. Yes, we. Something of the same order of things was done to the aboriginal Irish in the 16th and 17th centuries. But going back and undoing history — "give Ireland back to the aboriginal Irish" — is absurd. We can undo some of the consequences of history, and surely we should, but that is all.

A. "The Irish" have taken it back!

B. Come to think of it, was that a good thing?

A. Yes, it was. I agree that there are tragic things in history which nonetheless in fact entered importantly into historical progress. They are a large part of what Marxists think of as human "pre-history" — the history of class society. They can't be undone or reversed and they shouldn't be if they could: their effects have entered into and shaped irreversible histories. The English plunder and attempts at genocide of my ancestors in Ireland played a part in the primitive accumulation of English capital, which revolutionised the world, Ireland too, eventually, and for the better. We can wish that things had been done less murderously and with fewer victims. At this remove we can only try to mend some of the consequences.

B. With democracy. As we do.

A. Democracy itself worked to destroy the Amerindians. The Native Americans did much better in Canada and even in parts of Central and South America, even though terrible things were done to them there, than in the USA. In the USA there was no authoritative central state (like the British power in Canada or the Spanish power in South America). There was no government which would have had the power, if it had the will, to coerce the settlers who repeatedly invaded territory allotted by treaty to the Native Americans, in pursuit of gold and good land.

B. OK. We've all seen the Western movies!

A. The democratic, self-governing, weak-state aspects of US society worked to create a relentless pressure on native-American territories and their Amerindian peoples. As you say, it's the sort of thing you see in many old Western movies.

B. Unpleasant. An oft-repeated tragedy. It can't be undone, and in its fundamentals shouldn't be.

A. No. But note the part played in the tragedy of the Amerindians by the democratic nature of society in the territory of the USA. The expulsion of the "civilised tribes" was the work of President Andrew Jackson, whose elevation was part of the expansion and social deepening of US democracy.

B. All right. Democracy enables, but it does not ennoble. It does not necessarily produce the ideal good society, or, always, the best behaviour. But if you are not against democracy, why do you point to its weaknesses?

A. I want to discuss democracy in history, and the history of democracy, because I want to deflate your mystical, a-historical notions of democracy as something always benign and always equal to its best self. There are many democracies in history. We fight for a democracy better than democracy in history so far, because it will be the self-rule of the lowest class in society, the working class, which will exploit and oppress no-one.

B. Women and black people and Amerindians eventually got the vote — a stake and a role in US democracy. Democracy was improved, adapted, and expanded. It evolved according to its benignly democratic nature.

A. But the USA's transformation was not just a peaceful evolution, a mere "democratic process". The slave states weren't quiet and passive passengers in the American body politic, waiting to be sorted out by democratic evolution. They shaped US foreign policy for a long time. We read of the American "Texicans'" fight for freedom in Texas against the Mexican military dictator Santa Ana.

B. Seen that film, too. Remember the Alamo!

A. In fact one of the grievances of American-Texicans like Jim Bowie against Mexico was that it forbade the black slavery that they wanted to introduce, and did introduce when they had control. They were not just martyrs in the fight of Americans in Texas for democratic self-rule. They were martyrs in the cause of extending slavery beyond the borders of the existing American slave states. You haven't seen that film yet...

B. That was then. This is the democratic now!

A. It took a very bloody civil war to free the slaves. And then, after less than a decade following the civil war in which the Federal government encouraged "Black Reconstruction", the political and social emancipation of the freed slaves, the ex-slaves were again plunged down into helotry. In practice they were deprived of the vote for a hundred years. Then it took the great civil rights struggles — initiated by a brave pioneering black woman, Rosa Parks, who in 1955 refused to give her seat on a bus to a white man as she was by law obliged to — to begin to give substance to the formal democratic rights of African-Americans and end segregation, or at least some aspects of segregation. The post-slavery century of black helotry is a terrible story. African-Americans are still having to fight right now against being casually shot down in the street by nervous cops.

B. Nevertheless, democracy and liberty allow progress. A civil rights movement was possible.

A. Yes. I don't say otherwise. But can we get back to the point I was trying to make? The "good things" in the early American democracy were designed for a society of small and medium producers. Thomas Jefferson thought slavery would simply wither away. But that was before the 19th century expansion of the Lancashire cotton trade, the world's most advanced power-driven industry, and the consequent expansion of the market for slave-produced raw cotton on which Britain's Lancashire cotton mills depended.

The physiognomy of society changed, and at an accelerated pace after the Civil War. Giant industrial enterprises emerged — railroads, mines, oil, steel, cars, etc. In a democracy designed for 18th century communities of small and medium-sized producers (and small and medium slave-owners), these giants and their owners bestrode society like the proverbial Colossus.

B. So, society evolves. Do you want to stop that?

A. I want you to understand what happened to US democracy as a result of those social changes.

B. You want to devalue, disqualify, and disparage actually existing democracy. That's what you are trying to do!

A. I want you to see that US social evolution has devalued and disparaged and in effect disqualified its original democratic ideal, and to an enormous extent.

Women march for the vote in early 20th century Britain: in some advanced capitalist countries that right was not won until the 1970s. Below: the Chartists use their mass petition as a battering-ram to try to force working-class representation into Parliament.

Women And Democracy

A. You know, of course, that even in the most democratic countries, women were long excluded from democracy and from equal citizenship? A woman had no vote, no right to personal property as against her husband, no rights with her children. That was the underside of the great democratic progress for humankind over centuries. The political and social "rights of man and the citizen" which were won, more or less, in the French Revolution and the other bourgeois revolutions did not exist for women for many decades after they existed for men, or at least for some men. Women have had to fight for their own "bourgeois" revolution. And that fight is still going on.

B. No, democracy prevails.

A. If it does, it didn't come to prevail peacefully. Women had to fight, and some women to die, to win even approximations to equality and democracy.

B. That crazy suffragette, Emily Davison, throwing herself under the hooves of the king's horse at a racetrack? Advance for women would have come anyway, as a result of their role in the factories during the First World War.

A. Don't be such a bonehead! Women workers were exploited as workers, and doubly exploited as workers on lower rates of pay than men, even for the same jobs. They were triply exploited, because they were without substantial political and social rights.

B. Letting women into many jobs previously the preserve of men liberated them.

A. It opened up great possibilities, while also systematically blocking off their realisation. Capitalism primed people to fight for the equality it promised but could not deliver. Women have had to fight a double fight. Women need socialism as much as men, maybe more so. To an enormous extent, in practice unequal pay continues. So does the channelling of women workers into usually lower-paid jobs. So do glass ceilings. So does the main burden of child-care and housework.

B. Modern domestic equipment and fast food shops, all products of capitalism, have already "liberated" women.

A. Not even remotely enough! To liberate women fully, socialism would reorganise domestic work on a collective basis, amongst other changes.

B. Capitalism has already done some real things to lighten the load. Why do you think the working class would do more?

A. Because most women are working class, and in a general forward movement of the whole working class, the female half of the class would want to liberate itself fully. It would cut away the barriers which restrict women's equality outside the home. Women's status would rise.

B. Some people think it has risen enough. Spectacularly, in fact.

A. There are many things still to fight for: equal pay; equal respect; free, state-of-the-art health care that meets women's needs; safe pregnancy, safe childbirth, safe abortion; freely available social childcare.

B. Isn't there a choice to be made between your socialism on the one hand, and feminism, anti-racism, etc. on the other? Anti-socialists can and do believe in feminism and anti-racism. You are trying to boost your socialism by selling it as something else. If you were really sure of your socialism, you would concentrate on that. Logically, you should argue against women's organisations on the grounds that they divide the workers' movement.

A. Then we'd be your ideal socialists? Narrow, stupid, and not in touch with real life and the problems of real people. Socialists are honest participants in the battles of women, black people, refugees, and others, because what their zealots fight for is part of what we fight for. There is a logical and natural link between their battles and our socialism. In any case, it is not really "us" and "them": "they" are an equal part of our people, of the human and working-class solidarity for which we fight.

Feminism, concern with what used to be called "the woman question" or "the rights of women", was submerged for decades before writers like Simone de Beauvoir, Kate Millett, Betty Friedan and others recharged its ideological batteries and a women's movement began again in the 1960s. During the decades of feminist eclipse, there was, I think, only one text in continuous circulation on the left that dealt with "the woman question" from the point of view of liberating women. What do you think that was?

B. It can't have been a socialist text, anyway. You people jumped on the feminist bandwagon.

A. It was Leon Trotsky's book on Stalinist Russia, *The Revolution Betrayed*, published in 1936-7. As well as the other horrors and crimes of the Stalinist counter-revolution, Trotsky indicted the destruction of the women's rights and freedoms won in the Russian workers' revolution. In the form of a critique of the counter-revolution in relation to women, Trotsky expounded and championed the liberation of women. Read the chapter on "Family, Youth, and Culture". It was a central part of the Bolshevik critique of Stalinism, and a central part of the anti-Stalinist Bolshevik left.

B. Whatever. The idea that women in Britain today are oppressed is wild exaggeration. Demagogy. Socialists who were serious in their socialism would have no truck with such ideas.

A. Only bigoted fools would oppose campaigns for women's rights, or against oppression of gay people, or against racism, or denounce activists in such campaigns with the claim that their activity is "divisive". Serious fighters for solidarity get involved, help the campaigns to grow or initiate them, and contribute to political discussions about how best to go forward. These are complementary parts of the socialist cause of solidarity in society, not alternatives.

B. When we had a good woman as prime minister, bigoted socialists spat hate at her. What were they — what were you — if not anti-woman?

A. Thatcher was a disgrace to womankind as well to humanity. She offered negative proof that "womanism" is not enough in a world where women are part of the bourgeoisie as well as of the exploited class, the working class. If not proof, at least evidence that "womanism" — feminism that is not socialist — cannot finally emancipate women. The women's "bourgeois" revolution must be fused with the general socialist revolution if it is to win its great liberating objectives.

Fighters in the Warsaw Ghetto rising of April-May 1943, when the beleaguered Jewish community, under the leadership of socialists including left Zionists, rose up against the Nazi army occupying the city. Below: Women of the mining villages march during the miners' strike, 1984-5, in a mobilisation of the entire working-class population.

How Secure Is Democracy?

A. As I've said, your lack of democratic ambition now may prove to be suicidal. For democracy such as we have it, I mean.
B. I don't want to risk tinkering with what we have for fear of making things worse. *That* is suicide?
A. Your attitude to capitalism and bourgeois democracy is: stand fast, cherish what we have of democracy — bourgeois democracy — and worship it! See no fault, speak of no fault, hear of no fault! Like the "three wise monkeys"!
B. Don't risk undermining it and destroying it.
A. That sort of argument depends on the premiss that bourgeois democracy is stable and self-sustaining, that we have reached a plateau in social and historical evolution and will stay there. Have we though? Look ahead a little.
B. No! Look around you! Democracy has spread across the world since the collapse of the USSR in 1991. Many authoritarian governments have vanished like weird nightmares when the morning sun begins to shine. It's an aspect of the spread of capitalism across the world — what someone has called "the New Enlightenment". Mass demonstrations have faced down unpopular governments. The new social media have boosted the power of ideas and given everyone a "voice" that carries across the globe.
A. All that is true as far as it goes, and good. But are you sure democracy is stable? In the longer term, I mean.
B. Why shouldn't it be? It's immensely valuable. People know that.
A. Why should it be? It has this tremendous San Andreas-scale fault-line running through it: the political system is at odds with the property system. The contradiction can be blurred in "creative ambiguity" or held under control, but not always and not forever. There is a notional system of democratic rule in societies run in fact by plutocrats and serving their interests, which are not necessarily the same, and certainly not always the same, as those of the electorate. Rooted in that contradiction already is the lying and demagogy which rots our political system, and which handles major political questions (ecology is the great modern example) by trivialising them, by denying facts, by bamboozling, by lying. In the USA most of the media and virtually all the politicians work to preserve and exploit the crying ignorance of so much of the electorate.

B. But according to you that "fault-line" is there now, when democracy has spread across the world. Why shouldn't that remain stable, the established norm?

A. The tide of progress can be reversed. At the start of the 20th century, people in Europe believed in unending progress. Things could only get better, and would get better, by degrees. There had been a hundred years of more or less peace, of only relatively marginal and small wars in Europe. Trade had expanded. Many diseases were no longer devastating. The big countries of Europe were knit together by interlinking monarchies and aristocracies. Capitalism, applied reason, and expanding democracy would ensure endless peace, progress, and ever-expanding prosperity. People had greater hopes and expectations for an ever-improving future than most today dare to have. Many countries that would later reintroduce it had abolished the death penalty. And you know what happened then. Europe was engulfed in an inter-imperialist war in which millions died or were injured. The world system was dislocated. Production fell dramatically in the great slump after 1929. Then came the Second World War, during which something like 60 million people died. Giant factories for killing millions and million of people and disposing of the bodies; large parts of Europe in ruins.

B. People learn. Capitalists learn. The "general will" asserts itself. General economic interpenetration of countries develops, and brings stability and peace.

A. That sort of argument could have been made equally in 1914 or in 1939. Reason does not always prevail. Why? Because there are conflicting "reasons", rooted conflicts of interest that can be resolved only by force. By economic force, as things are now, but ultimately also by military force. There are still great powers, though not always the same great powers as in the 20th century, jockeying on behalf of conflicting interests and drives and necessities. There are actual and potential conflicts.

And it isn't just a matter of future breakdown. In many of the nominally democratic countries, "democracy" is shallow and insubstantial even compared to democracy in Britain which, as you know, I think, has a lot wrong with it, and lacks the expansiveness of a full, socialist, democracy. Large parts of the world are in the grip of strands of political Islam, of varying degrees of intensity and malignancy and often hostile to each other, but, every one of them, reactionary and regressive. Even a few decades ago that irruption in strength from the dark ages would have seemed impossible. Your picture of democracy's present prosperity is not quite true. It is also possible, though I won't pursue it further here, to imagine not too far ahead a future troubled by ecological crises and disasters. The consequent social and national strains and stresses and conflicts might well break the balancing mechanisms which allow plutocratic democracy to live with its inherent contradictions.

B. Democracy is a great power in the world now! I mean, the idea of it, commitment to it. That won't go away easily.

A. Which doesn't mean it won't break down. They were so committed to peace in 1914 that they found a "war to end all wars". In the early 1990s some talked of the "end of history": who would then have credited the scale of the rise of political Islam since?

B. Democracy is the idea whose time has come and for which conditions are right. It is the idea that has power because it has gripped the masses.

A. There is a great deal of wishful thinking in what you say and your picture of reality is faulty. The rising great power, China, combines old Stalinist rule with capitalism in a way which is as near to fascism as it can be — a new fascistic synthesis. The "Communist Party of China" is going the way that the Guomindang (GMD) of Chiang Kai Shek went, whose rule the Maoists overthrew in 1949. The GMD began as a revolutionary party and was, with the help of Russian advisers, organised like a Stalinist party. It became a gangster power-cartel. The combination of private capitalist and Stalinist authoritarianism is, in every way and every field, as far from democracy as you can get. The system in Russia is not much more than notionally democratic. At best "democracy" — actually existing bourgeois democracy — is shallow. It can be uprooted. Progress can be reversed, as in the first half of the 20th century it was. That San Andreas fault of capitalism, the contradiction between notional majority rule and actual economic rule by a small minority, can shatter bourgeois democracy again.

B. If that "San Andreas fault" between democracy and the economic system existed, yes it might. It doesn't exist. Anyway, democracy has strong foundations. It will stand any shocks.

A. In 1973, a military coup against a mildly socialist government destroyed democracy in Chile, one of the oldest parliamentary democracies in the world.

B. Latin America! Britain isn't a banana republic!

A. Neither was Chile. In February 1974 some "fairly senior" British army officers discussed a coup in Britain. The then Chief of Staff, Michael

Carver, admitted it in public some years later (see the *Guardian* of 5 March 1980).

B. It didn't get very far, did it?

A. I suppose you know what the Mandarin-Maoist one-time Chinese prime minister Zhou Enlai is supposed to have said when he was asked if the French revolution of 1789-94 had been a success.

B. I don't.

A. He answered: "It is too early to say". In the sweep of history democracy is so far little more than a tentative and still too shallowly rooted growth. It will remain that, at best, so long as the contradiction between the bourgeois-democratic political structures and the system of private property exists. If we miss the historical chance to put democracy on a sustainable basis, that is to bring the system of property in the means of production into line with the political structures, then it may go, and come back never or only at some unforeseeable future historical juncture.

B. Your warped view of capitalism, which in history is the progenitor of democracy, makes you see contradictions as absolute and irreconcilable which in fact are not irreconcilable and not absolute.

A. Bias towards desired conclusions is, true, a factor in all debate and discussion. Serious people try to watch that in themselves, and to avoid it — to "factor in" their own bias, and take account of it. You don't seem able to do that. Why? Capitalism is a product of history. History has produced other systems too — the slave system of antiquity, Asiatic despotism, feudalism, Stalinist bureaucratic collectivism. You think capitalism is the "natural" system, that it corresponds to "human nature", and that there is not much, or nothing overwhelmingly, wrong with either the economic or the political system, or with their relationship to each other? But history has known some fearful and unexpected turns: the one in the early decades of the 20th century, to stick with that example. I conclude that even bourgeois democracy is good, but only socialism, resolving the contradiction between political majority rule and economic minority rule, can win and secure multi-dimensional — economic, social, political — democracy.

B. I have a true-to-life picture of the world we live in. I measure capitalism against the past. You measure it against an imagined future, so that the real faults of capitalism are compared to an ideal. Naturally capitalism is found wanting.

A. To see, even if only for the sake of argument, the faults of capitalism, the inner contradictions of bourgeois democracy, and the tremendous

HOW SECURE IS DEMOCRACY?

possibilities inherent in the potential created by capitalism — and then try to waffle them away, is, I suggest, breathtakingly irresponsible. You say you measure capitalism and bourgeois democracy by the past, and therefore find them tremendous and beautiful. But if you didn't measure them like that, you couldn't be so complacent and so smug.

B. No. Beautiful is your word, not mine.

The Bryant and May match workers, in East London, who helped spark mass trade-unionism in Britain in the late 19th century. Below, left to right: Robert Owen, starting as a wealthy employer, helped organise the labour movement; Louise Michel, an anarchist, was a heroine of the Paris Commune; Jim Larkin organised workers in Belfast and Dublin.

French workers march against laws imposing more "flexibility" on the labour market, 2017. The placards say: "Lose your life earning your living", and "I work/ You work/ He or she works/ We work/ You work/ They profit".

Part 6: Capitalism and the "Invading Socialist Society"

The "Invading Socialist Society"

B. Your claim that Marxist socialism is rational and "scientific", not merely utopian, is just a dream — pure delusion. An empty conceit.

A. Karl Marx once defined his socialism as a consciousness of the unconscious social processes. It is a good description. Socialism — political, social, and economic communality, generalised human solidarity and fellowship — is of course a good idea. It always has been. It was a good idea hundreds of years and millennia before Karl Marx. Marxists called themselves "scientific socialists" because their socialism was more than a mere good idea about how things might be and should be. It was an idea of how the economy, society, and human thinking about how to organise social life, were in sober fact tending to go. How they were compelled by their own logic to go. An idea of how the contradictions in capitalist society would propel society forward.

B. You have an impressive capacity to fool yourself, and to go on fooling yourself.

A. Marx and Engels grasped the underlying tendency of capitalism to develop from smaller to ever larger concentrations of capital. Today we have reached the stage of global corporations so powerful that they can sometimes override governments and they ordinarily exercise a great deal of control over them. Routinely they evade the control of elected governments. Often they avoid paying taxes. They have the economic and political strength of medium-sized states. In certain boardrooms, the elect of capitalist civilisation can decide to move whole industries, employing thousands of workers, from one country to another, in search of cheaper labour-power or more docile workers.

B. But they are controlled by us all through the market.

A. The market is a good enough substitute for democracy?

B. Political control over all these economic operations is impossible. To attempt it would bring only bureaucratic bungling. The market may not be a perfect mechanism, but it works to make sure that economic activity serves the majority.

A. Capitalism socialises and centralises the processes of production, of exchange, and of communication. The plans and policies of a small number of companies govern what happens to many tens of millions of people. In the 18th century great commercial entities like the British East India Company fought wars — sometimes against their French or Dutch equivalents — and conquered countries such as India. They ran ahead of governments. We have not quite come full circle here, but we aren't all that far from it either.

Frederick Engels once spoke of this phenomenon of capitalism's inbred tendency and need to "socialise" production, when it was at a very early stage compared to now, as "the invading socialist society". The mechanism of capitalism itself is the main engine of the evolution of capitalism towards socialism. It prepares society for socialism by its component units' relentless drives for growth, profit, monopolisation, annexation, the eating-up of competitors.

Marx's view was right or wrong as a picture of the social and economic reality of capitalism, as an expectation and advocacy about where it could go and could be made to go. But there was nothing vague and undefined about it, no arbitrary project-mongering, no utopianism. *That* was why we call ourselves "scientific socialists".

B. Alchemistic socialists, surely! It has a better ring to it. And it's true.

A. You need to prattle less, and think about things a little more! Socialism is the anticipatory shadow that capitalism casts ahead of itself.

B. Capitalism never approximates the state monopoly system you want. No matter how big a corporation gets to be, there are competing corporations. Even giant corporations can go bust.

A. Yes. But some of today's global corporations control as much already as a whole developed country's government could a hundred years ago by nationalising industry. Some of the big and medium superstores contain whole towns'-worths of shops, organised and brought under one roof. But let me continue.

This state of affairs means that a tremendous degree of socialisation of the means of production, exchange, and communication already exists now. Each of the giant international conglomerates is a sort of island of "socialism", that is, of a planned economy. All this is the bedrock for our advocacy of socialism now. Socialists criticise pluto-democracy because it can't function as the multi-dimensional democracy that is required by these developments. The running of the great corporations needs to be put under democratic control. Here, democracy and socialism merge.

B. That is nonsensical! These corporations, no matter how big they are,

are run for the private profit of the owners. They are avowedly, undisguisedly capitalist.

A. Exactly!

B. They are governed by the self-interest, as they perceive it, of the office holders and shareholders. They are run democratically too. Each share carries a vote.

So too is the whole economy run democratically. Each purchase, so to speak, is a vote which almost mechanically regulates supply and demand in the economy.

A. In the market, the rich have much more "voting power" than the rest of us! But you think everything is for the best, in the best world you can imagine? Then how came the depression of 2007-8 and after...?

B. It is better than the world you imagine and advocate and say you "fight" for, and what socialism comes to in reality — Stalinism, or some similar -ism.

A. The point is that present-day capitalist reality has created mountains of evidence for the basic Marxist thesis on which everything else depends — the spontaneous concentration of capital into gigantic social entities. Even Marx might be momentarily astonished at the extent of it now and the continued growth of the scope of the multinational corporations. You are loud in insisting that you are a democrat, yet you glory in the fact that these tremendous enterprises operate outside democratic control of any sort and for the private profit of a few...

B. Only to show that they have nothing to do with socialism! These things are capitalist.

A. Yes, they are capitalist. No denying that! No-one who knows what socialism or capitalism is would say otherwise. You glory in the fact that these great social and economic engines are run for the benefit of private interests.

B. That's the only possible economic basis of democracy.

A. Each big corporation is, so to speak, an island of democracy! You think the corporations are democratically run by the shareholders? And you conclude that that makes the whole thing democratic, the totality of multinationals and conglomerates? In fact, as everyone knows, the great "socialised" capitalist enterprises are dominated by the owners of big concentrations of capital, not by a demos of small and very small investors.

B. There are "shareholder revolts".

A. Not many, and not decisively. In any case, even if "shareholder" democracy were real, it is a strange idea that the system is made democratic as a whole by some elements being internally democratic, no matter how many of those there are. You probably know that the Caribbean pirates in the 17th and 18th centuries, who roamed the seas robbing, burning, and murdering, sometimes organised their shipboard communities democratically, discussing and deciding big questions by vote. I never heard of anybody who argued that therefore they were not pirates, or that their shipboard democracy should be reckoned as a contribution to the progress of democracy in the world.

B. The equation of the great commercial enterprises of today to those pirates is ludicrous! They operate legally, not outside the law.

A. Do they? In fact they make and remake law, or flout and ignore it. Essentially, it is their law. We have yet to see one of these pirates hanged in chains at Marble Arch, the site of the old-time hanging ground, Tyburn!

B. But their rule is not a lawless tyranny

A. Tell that to communities suddenly deprived of jobs by ukase of an international corporation seeking higher profits or more docile and more exploitable workers. Often, now, the rule of the corporations is a lawless tyranny. My point here, though, is that the development of the giant corporations has greatly strengthened the Marxist idea, that capitalism by its own operation, on its own laws of motion, erects the mechanical underpinnings of the future socialist economy.

B. The viability of the existing social, political, and economic system within which the concentration of capital takes place — that is what kills socialism!

A. But it isn't dead! In relation to the "social" character of the big corporations and conglomerates, what needs to be done was spelled out as long ago as 1848 by Karl Marx and Frederick Engels in the Communist Manifesto: the working class has to "win the battle of democracy".

B. We — all of us, not just the working class — have won the battle of democracy already!

A. The world around you shows that that is not so. Most of the things that shape our lives are outside democratic control. International corporations make that more not less true. They can even decide what taxes they will deign to pay. They act in some ways like sovereign states.

B. We'll see.

A. We'll see. The widespread post-Stalinist sentiment against socialism solves nothing basic for capital. Capitalism exists objectively. Its inner traits, its laws operate objectively and go on operating. The fundamental political contradiction is that these comparatively few corporations, run for their owners' private profit, control the economy of the vast world wide society which everyone depends on and lives in, and they are largely outside democratic control. The gobbledegook about democratic corporations does not change that one bit. In the great slump that began in 2007-8, people saw governments act to intervene and subsidise giant banks. We haven't "won the battle of democracy" yet; but we will.

B. You're whistling in the dark.

A. This is, for Marxists, the "objective" basis of our socialism. It operates, and goes on operating, no matter how weak or confused the forces conscious of the logic and needs of this process — the socialists — are. It is only with the help of the conscious activity of socialists that we can win the harmonious outcome of these social contradictions and dynamics. But the dynamic which creates the preconditions for socialism goes on working even amidst the massacre of the socialists, and even if it is administered by those who condemn socialism or massacre socialists. All they achieve, all they can achieve, is to limit the solution of the social contradictions, for a time, to stop-gap, pro-tem expedients like those taken in 2007-8 and after. In recent times it has been the driving force behind globalisation, the concentration of the means of production, distribution, and communication into gigantic, and ever yet more gigantic, enterprises.

Today, across the world, there are enormous conglomerates of means of production, exchange, and communication, in corporations that relate to the existing states something like the smaller Duke and prince ruled sub-states of the Dark Ages and the Middle Ages to the monarchies to which they nominally owed allegiance. The corporations' autonomy vis-a-vis national states increases as their strength increases.

These modern "commercial kingdoms" operate as lawless tyrannies to those who work within them, and as looting brigands to the societies around them. All this is rooted in the spontaneous movement of the capitalist productive forces into ever bigger concentrations. To change the image, it is like a pool of piranha fish who over time eat each other up until there are far fewer, but bigger and fatter, piranha fish left. The contradictions that have grown in the two centuries since the Industrial Revolution from the continued private ownership and operation of the social means of production do not lessen but become more acute. So do its ingrained perpetual conflicts with the bulk of the people.

German Communist Party poster, 1925: All out for international women's day on 8 March! Against imperialist war! Into the red united front!

Planning: Who Plans? In Whose Interests?

B. "Planning" is still your answer: the old socialist panacea. But you can't "plan" a complex modern economy in every detail. The attempt to do that creates an enormous and inevitably incompetent bureaucracy, not a usable plan.

A. It is not a matter of plan or no plan. The great corporations have their plans, too. The issue is who plans, and in whose interest — the interests of society, or of the rich and super-rich?

B. No, the issue is between modest sectional plans by the great corporations, and an overblown, state-wide, cauterising, totalitarian, socialist economic plan.

A. This is a curious case of a myth erected upon a myth. Here too, there is a sly substitution of something else for what is supposedly being discussed.

Planning of every detail is impossible? Yes, I think that is true. Therefore? Therefore the exploitation that is central to capitalism, as to different modes of exploitation are to all class societies, cannot be done away with? Therefore the mad superstition rules that the market must be treated as a god that can be overruled only at risk of catastrophe? That idea parallels the notion that socialists are against private property, and would, therefore, seize your house and your smartphone, when in fact socialists are only against private property in the means of production and the exploitation that goes with it. Both ideas are beside the point.

You say that because it would be impossible to pre-plan all the complex details of a modern economy, therefore all planning is entirely impossible. Thereby you evade the decisive questions: Who plans? What is to be planned? What needs to be planned? How much needs to be planned if we are to escape the tyranny of the market and the capitalist class exploitation that goes with it?

Socialism does not need or presuppose a Stalinist-like "planning" or attempted planning of everything. It doesn't need the nationalisation of everything, either. What needs to be planned and integrated into coherence are the great basic decisions of production and distribution. There is no reason why in such planning there cannot also be free choice of what individuals consume, and production that is responsive to what people like or want.

Limited markets in a socialist society would be a mechanism to establish, register, and regulate such things. Markets would complement socialist planning, and be one of its tools.

B. In fact the socialist "planned economies" were not responsive to demand.

A. That was because of the totalitarian Stalinist political system. The Stalinists nationalised everything down to the proverbial corner shop because the Stalinist ruling class, the bureaucratic class, demanded for itself every possible scrap of wealth, in the painfully underdeveloped society over which they ruled. They viewed small enterprises as class competition from "the petty bourgeoisie" for a part of the surplus product.

B. What's that, the surplus product, when it's at home?

A. All that can be leeched out of the producers; for the working class, all the value they add in their work, above the cost of their wages.

B. You mean the legitimate returns on investment!

A. No, I mean the exploitation of workers! Trotsky and his comrades such as Christian Rakovsky severely criticised the "nationalisation" of everything in the USSR as socially cauterising. They also criticised the blindly-bureaucratic, over-detailed, handed-down-from-above Stalinist attempts at planning. Trotsky described the command economy created by Stalinism in the first half of the 1930s as an exercise governed by "bureaucratic delirium". Such measures were specific to Stalinism. They were never part of a Marxist programme. And, of course, to repeat, they were imposed by a totalitarian political regime and its state.

B. They could *only* be imposed by a totalitarian state. That will be as true of future attempts at a planned economy as of the Stalinist experience.

A. When Marxist socialists talk of planned economy, they mean, planned under a supremely democratic regime — democratically planned. The Stalinist "plan" in the USSR was the plan of a ruling bureaucratic class, not of the working class and the working people on whom it was imposed. Trotsky's objections to it were working-class criticisms of "planning" by the totalitarian state — criticism from the point of view of the victims of totalitarian planning.

B. Trotsky had no effect on what happened. He was like a cat thrown out into the cold, mewling angrily outside the door!

A. He represented and embodied old socialism, the socialism of the October revolution, and Bolshevism: read what he was "mewling"! The fact is that the great international and national conglomerates already plan now, for their own multifarious industries and networks.

B. Of course they do. That is why your "invading socialist society" is a delusion.

A. They plan. It is a fact. And a gigantic one here and now. It is evidence that there is such a thing as the "invading socialist society" at the heart of seemingly all-powerful capitalism. They plan — except that they plan for maximising markets and profits in competition with each other. They plan to get the greatest volume of profit. They plan, but the planning serves the interests of society only incidentally and on condition that it also serves their private interests. Socialist planning would integrate and make complementary the sectional capitalist planning that is a central attribute of modern capitalism, and reorient it to serve the interests of the people and of society as a whole. That way we would overcome the crying contradictions at the heart of capitalism: social production with private appropriation of the fruits of the productive labour of vast numbers of people. The running, and to some extent the planning, of giant conglomerates, on which society depends and in which millions work, for private gain, irrespective of social interests and social needs. I repeat: integrating and adapting the existing plans into human — as distinct from capitalist — coherence would not be all that difficult.

You're right that our capacity to predict is limited, and it is not possible to have a precise plan for every economic detail. But the argument for socialism does not depend in the least on future socialist economic plans being precise or minutely-detailed or error-free. It depends only on the claim that humanity can and must democratically and rationally plan the broad lines of the economic enterprises which now, after centuries of capitalist development, involve and affect us all, rather than leaving those broad lines to be decided by the outcome of chaotic competition driven by the greed of a few. As well as that basic argument, it is a fact that computers, which are continually being improved, do and will provide tremendous tools for planning.

B. Such an integrated central plan would inevitably lead to some species of authoritarianism. Increasing corporate power to plan points to the dangers. It is a danger that will increase, not lessen, with technological advance.

A. The question is not to plan or not to plan. It is not even one of what should or should not be centrally planned — but of who plans, how, and in whose interests. That is a question of democracy, of whether we continue to have the pluto-democracy we have now, or create a genuine three-dimensional democracy encompassing social, economic and political life. It is a question of whether or not the working class and the other working people "win the battle of democracy" against plutocratic bourgeois democracy.

The "End Gelände" ("Here and No Further") protests in 2016 and 2017 against Germany's increased burning of especially polluting coal, and terrain-blighting opencast mining, drew thousands from across Europe

Globalisation, Socialism, and Democracy

B. In any case, much of the old socialism was couched in terms of workers taking power in an existing state. Today the international conglomerates and the global financial markets are too much outside the power of national government for isolated national action to control an economy.

A. Yes, but also no. National governments do operate with cropped-down powers. Their economies are entwined with international economic operations over which they have little or no control. But national governments still have a lot of powers they don't use.

B. So, world government has to be in place first for a socialist transformation of even one country to be possible.

A. You should try to be consistent. Relate what you have just said to your claim that we already have a serviceable democracy, or maybe even the best possible democracy.

B. International conglomerates and global financial markets diminish democracy, true. But they do not destroy it — as socialists would.

A. No, we would expand and deepen democracy to take on the international conglomerates and the global financial markets! The problem you raise is new only in its form. Socialism have always conceived of working-class revolution as an international revolution. Wherever it started – France, Germany, Britain, or Russia – it would spread across Europe, at least. That is what the Bolsheviks aimed to initiate: an international working-class revolution.

It is inconceivable that the political ferment that would lead to a workers' revolution in, say, France, would not also affect the workers in neighbouring countries; inconceivable that a working-class revolution in one country would not spur workers in other countries to do the same by lighting up perspectives and possibilities the workers had not seen before. And do that much faster now, with modern communications.

B. Yet that didn't happen for the Bolsheviks in 1917 and after, did it?

A. In fact it did, most notably in Germany in 1918-19. Pro-Bolshevik movements, strong or weak, emerged all over Europe. Short-lived soviet governments were established in Hungary and Bavaria in 1919. Factory occupations covered Italy in 1920. The workers were defeated, in large part because of the politics and character of their leaderships. There is never a guarantee of victory, but it would be very unlikely that a socialist revolution, wherever it started, would be isolated in one country for long. It would not be an isolated socialist state in a sea of capitalist power, or not for long. Relatively recent history shows a number of examples of revolutions spreading from country to country — in Eastern Europe during the collapse of the Russian empire in 1989 and after, in the Arab world in 2011. In your own way, you are right for once. Wherever a socialist revolution started, it would have to become an international revolution. Yes!

B. Instant world government or nothing! Another tall order.

A. A world government is not going to happen soon (or maybe, if capitalism were to continue, ever). The emergence of a bloc of countries where the working class has set up socialist workers' governments is the likely great next step.

B. That's inconceivable — the remaining capitalist powers would be too hostile.

A. They were hostile to Bolshevik Russia. No fewer than 14 states intervened on the side of the counter-revolutionaries in the civil war that followed the 1917 revolution. But there was great working-class resistance to that at home in the countries that intervened. In 1920 British dockworkers refused to load munitions for the Polish army at war with revolutionary Russia.

B. Wishful thinking!

A. Precedent! Illuminating precedent.

B. The Bolsheviks remained isolated. You people offer that as explanation for what you call the Stalinist degeneration of the USSR.

A. Before the Russian revolution, during it, and after it, we advocated international socialist revolution.

B. What if your revolution remained internationally isolated?

A. Then we would be defeated. But neither precedent nor probability says defeat would be inevitable.

B. You refuse to face up to the new conditions of international capitalist power, and the new arguments against socialism which flow from them.

A. I'd say that the growth of new global oligarchies outside even notional democratic control creates new arguments for socialism, not against it. Your arguments against socialism are not new. For instance, in Britain in the mid-1920s, in a polemic with Leon Trotsky over Trotsky's book *Where is Britain Going?*, Bertrand Russell rejected the idea of a British working-class revolution because Britain was so heavily dependent on foreign trade. He argued that a working-class Britain would be isolated and crushed.

B. Russell was just being responsible.

A. Not to the fight for socialism, to which he paid some lip-service in its reform-socialist form. In fact a British working-class revolution would probably have detonated similar revolutions in Germany, France, and Italy. Today, as I've said, a working-class revolution in one country would light up the world as the Bolshevik revolution did, only faster and more brilliantly, and let millions see new possibilities and act to achieve them.

In Germany, abortion was almost always illegal, under section 218 of the constitution, until the 1970s. 1924 KPD poster by Käthe Kollwitz opposing the anti-abortion laws.

Advertising poster for the German Communists' daily "Red Flag", edited by Karl Liebknecht and Rosa Luxemburg

Part 7: What's In It For Me?

The Shit Jobs

B. You talk about an idyllic future where everyone shares and shares alike and cares for everyone else. But who will do the shit jobs in socialist society? Who will clean the toilets, collect the rubbish, look after the hopelessly mad, the incontinent old?

A. Self-cleaning toilets have been commonplace for decades. In reality, most such work can be done now, or soon, by machines, robots, etc.

B. Old dodderers like you will be cared for by machines? And babies? That's your humane socialist solution? Aren't you "magicking" away, in words, a real problem? Even the most automated society will never eliminate all the unpleasant jobs.

A. Then they will be shared out. Isn't your objection best expressed as: "Who would spend their whole working lives cleaning the lavatories?" Isn't it? That is what makes the thing truly horrible: that some people for all their lives should do nothing else but the shit jobs, and others, the good jobs.

Oscar Wilde put it well: "To sweep a slushy crossing for eight hours, on a day when the east wind is blowing is a disgusting occupation. To sweep it with mental, moral, or physical dignity seems to me to be impossible. To sweep it with joy would be appalling. Man is made for something better than disturbing dirt."

B. He was a socialist?

A. He was. One of the oddest things in our world, if you stand back and look at it, is that the good, interesting, capacity-employing, and developing, jobs are better paid than the bad, uninteresting, life-stifling jobs. Leave aside the obscene amounts of money that go to footballers and pop stars. The bankers and speculators and asset-strippers — social cockroaches, thieving magpies, rats, wolves, and jackals like that — swim in money. A surgeon who does interesting, rewarding, satisfying work earns so much more than the dirt-stirrer, the lavatory cleaner, the rubbish collector, whose working lives are almost devoid of satisfactions, and often very unpleasant as well as badly paid. In a humane, rational world, inhabited by equal people, the lavatory cleaner should have the high wage, in consideration of the damage, the suffering, the frustrating and dehumanising effects of the work, and the surgeon, who gets so much out of the work itself, the lesser wage.

B. That's economics for you!

A. That's capitalist economics for you. In reality the wage is regulated by the social costs of producing and reproducing the labour power of different jobs — what, respectively, it costs to train a surgeon and a lavatory cleaner — and by handed-down status.

B. It "shouldn't" be like that, but it is. Besides, don't forget that the surgeon will be a lot cleverer than the road-sweeper.

A. Not necessarily. Not usually. Just better educated.

B. Sentimental paradox-juggling! It is natural that people of wealth are the surgeons, and that people like you should clean the lavatories...

A. In a moral socialist world everybody could train to be a surgeon, or a classical musician, or a mathematician, or anything they want to be.

B. And some of those will sometimes clean the lavatories, or do similar menial jobs? Don't be silly! Grow up!

A. Why not? The idea will disappear that some people are "too good", of too high a caste, too well-educated, their dignity too high, for them to do unpleasant work that other humans do. A socialist society will have a human ethos and morality. It will be governed by the central idea of human solidarity and intrinsic human worth. It will realise the great aspiration to human equality in society, in education, and in access to economic resources. It will thus lead to a flowering of things in which human beings are not and never can be entirely equal — capacity, interest, talent. It will provide for all the things that are now only for the well-off and the super-rich. It will enhance and develop every human life.

B. And the rivers will turn into lemonade, and some to champagne, and the socialist sturgeons will increase their production of eggs so that there will be caviare for everyone!

A. I've never had either. I don't know or care. But in principle, if some people want champagne and caviare, why not?

B. Scarcity! So they have to be rationed, and rationing by price is better than rationing by government decree, in which the governors will always make sure they get first pick and more than their fair share.

A. With technology as we have it now, most things don't need to be rationed at all. Food, clothes, public transport, for example: everyone could simply have what they want, and quite soon no-one would want excessive or wasteful consumption. Under capitalism, even in comparatively well-off Britain, one-third of lower-income parents skip meals in school holidays so that their children can eat, and hundreds of thousands have to ask for supplies from food banks, while a few dine in expensive restaurants. Of course, no way of organising society can enable everyone to live in the house with the best view. Some things will always be scarce. But why should that mean any more than that if you choose one scarce "prize", you must forego another? Why do you doubt that people can develop enough social solidarity and empathy to do that fairly? Attitudes change. As in, for example, the startling changes in sexual morality. Only five decades ago, the "conspicuous consumption" sort of sex life now available to more or less everybody who wants it in advanced capitalist societies was possible only for Hollywood film stars, some rich people, and small groups of libertines who believed in "free love" (you don't hear that expression any more. Why? It's from another world, vastly different to ours.)

B. Oh well, sex. That really is basic human nature!

A. The same human nature used to be suppressed and shackled by religion-based moral and social sex codes. As recently as 1988, Thatcher's Tory government legislated "Section 28", branding homosexuality as contrary to human nature and making it illegal to "promote the teaching in any maintained school of the acceptability of homosexuality". Attitudes have changed so much since then that in 2013 a Tory-led government legislated for same-sex marriage. (But they still haven't made sex education compulsory in schools). Or consider the changes in the forms of the family, in history and in recent times.

B. Progress, I suppose. But not everything can be changed.

A. Trotsky envisaged a world in which the average human being would be at the intellectual level of an Aristotle. Someone recently branded that as an element of romantic "utopianism" in Trotsky.

B. Or lunatic raving!

A. Who can say that it won't be so, still less that in terms of human capacity it can't be? We are still living in humankind's pre-history. History will not end, but this pre-history will. Humanity will rise to a level commensurate with our best benign possibilities and potentials. The citizen of that world will look back at ours as we look back on the stony cruelty and inhumanity of the ancient world, with its slaves, its gladiators killing each other for the citizens' enjoyment, its mass ignorance, its stultified means of producing and reproducing the necessities of human life.

Capitalism, Inventors, and Future Progress

B. The competitiveness and greed embedded in human nature can't be changed. And anyway shouldn't be. Without the stimulus of self-interest — greed for wealth, power, and status over and above other people — progress would grind to a halt. For instance, how are we going to discover new technologies, invent new procedures, make breakthroughs like penicillin or the internet or the microchip, if people do not have as stimulus the hope of riches and rewards? Without that everything would seize up.

A. It is a fact that under this system the hope of riches, prestige, and self-aggrandisement does spur people on to effort and perseverance. So does the fear of poverty and of being someone else's prey. Wages at the end of the week or month spur most people on to persevere, that is, to go to work! In a socialist society the knowledge of social necessity will spur people on. But if you think that wealth and power are the only spurs to action in humankind — my God, what a miserably diminished view you have of human beings! A mean bourgeois view. It is a piece of humanity-slandering bourgeois superstition! You think capitalism and its characteristic traits can be read off from human nature. The opposite is true: your idea of human nature and human potentials is read off from capitalist modes and moralities around you.

B. I take a realistic view of history, and of society now. and of human nature. Facts speak louder than limp-witted sentimentality

A. All right: first, I'll take your point on its own terms. I don't know that anything necessary to a socialist society or to the work of building such a society rules out giving special material rewards or prestige to people who contribute important inventions and innovations to society. That stimulus need not disappear with capitalism. Certainly it doesn't depend on the whole of society being run for the private profit of a small minority, very few of whom contribute new inventions or, indeed, anything very much. Consider the Nobel Prizes, which confer status and financial reward on people in many fields of endeavour — science, literature, politics, and for such intangible things as promoting "peace". How many people in all those fields work with the conscious objective of winning a Nobel Prize? How many would stop what they are doing when they know that they won't get one?

B. Maybe a lot of them: how do you know?

A. There is a Nobel Prize for poetry, awarded in the past to such as William Butler Yeats. Yeats certainly needed the money, but do you think it was the hope of money which spurred him on to do his wonderful work?

Or take penicillin, the discovery of which is attributed to Alexander Fleming, in 1928. In fact he made observations of the antibiotic properties of a mould, published his observations in a scientific journal, got little attention, and was unable to see how to mass-produce penicillin.

The development of penicillin as an effective medicine was the work of others, over a decade later, stimulated, empowered, accelerated by the great need for medicine in World War Two. The invention of antibiotics was not driven by expectations of wealth or status. It was driven by perceived need. It was production for need.

B. Fleming was eventually feted and knighted. He wasn't indifferent to such things, was he?

A. The point is that he was not spurred on or governed by the prospect of such things. The great work he initiated was not generated by hopes or expectations of money or glory. Or take a case more favourable to you: the great Thomas Edison, who ran a production-line for discoveries and new techniques. He was certainly greedy for money.

B. He was a great promoter of new inventions. Economic progress needs such entrepreneurs.

A. One of the reasons the nascent film industry moved from the East Coast of the USA to California was to escape the harassment of Edison's patent-enforcers. As you say, Edison was more an entrepreneur than an inventor. As a profit-hungry entrepreneur he was as likely to stifle inventions as to help them. That is what capitalist "entrepreneurs" do.

B. Still, Edison brought many inventions into practical use. He couldn't have done that without being the sort of profit-seeker you want to stifle and render impossible in your socialist Utopia.

A. I don't know, can't know, but it seems possible to me that the American Thomas Edison, or another Thomas Edison, in a socialist society, would gain satisfaction and pleasure and self-approbation from sheer enterprise, from the practical realisation of inventions he picked up from others. The American Thomas Edison...

B. The real Thomas Edison...

A. ... was, so to speak, psychologically plugged in to late 19th century and early 20th century US capitalism and its typical drives and motivations. What would someone of his talents, drive, and interests have been like in an older society, say in ancient Greece? Or in a future society? It is surely possible to imagine someone like him "plugged in" to a different psychology, different drives, different moralities, different motivations, different satisfactions, different standards of self-judgement and self-measurement. Social service, benevolence towards his fellow citizens, the desire for recognition as a benefactor of humankind?

B. Things are what they are. Edison was what he was. In a socialist world he and others like him would be stifled and made an impossibility.

A. Because of lack of financial reward? But, as I've said, there are no reasons why a socialist society could not offer special material rewards for exceptional services, a sort of Great Human Benefactor Prize.

B. You concede my point, then!

A. Rewards and honours for innovators are not an issue in the argument between socialism and capitalism. There can be different mechanisms for rewarding them, so long as people want that sort of thing.

B. Capitalism is the tried and tested way. It works. Your socialist system simply wouldn't work. It couldn't. It would stifle and destroy.

A. The paradoxical truth is that innovators who are unrecognised and unrewarded cogs in present-day institutionalised technology, science and research might well get more recognition and reward in a socialist society.

B. I may go to heaven when I die. But I'm not going to kill myself just to find out.

A. Your Heaven would be what? Eternity in a virtual bank counting imaginary money!

B. And yours? Sitting in a library dreaming up imaginary, impossible worlds.

A. Your mistake is to think in great conglomerate blocks of ideas and associations. You refuse to break them down, to analyse. You do not separate out what was and is from what could be. The real Thomas Edison, a product of a certain time and environment, was greedy, therefore only greed can drive any person with his interests, abilities and capacities. No: as we've seen, people are shaped by their social environment, by what society values and holds up for emulation. "Human nature" is socially malleable.

B. Yes, it can produce and license socialist...

A. Stalinist!

B. ... concentration camp guards and murderers.

A. Of course, but what licensed what they did was not socialism but the Stalinist counter-revolution against socialism. Ideas, drives, capacities are shaped, their innate traits encouraged or blocked, sublimated or diverted, by the different social and political regimes. Capitalism brings out, glorifies, rewards, and lauds the worst in people. But people are as capable of being gripped by benign drives and ideals of fellowship, social service, and, dare I say, empathy and love, as by the dog-eat-dog, war-of-all-against-all dreams of robbing their neighbours which capitalism conditions them into, from the cradle to the school to the workplace. Anyway, I think you have a false view of how science and scientific development work.

Research and development of drugs, for instance, is a large-scale capitalist activity. There is still sometimes the genius individual inventor or innovator. But mostly the development of science, inventions, and techniques is highly institutionalised and capitalised. That capitalist research and development is driven and regulated by the hope of gain — gain for the corporation and its shareholders, not for the inventors or for society in general, even though social benefits may ultimately come.

B. That makes no difference. Greed and selfishness rule. That is the point, whether we are talking of an individual inventor, or a whole corporation.

A. Do you really want to argue that the need to reward invention justifies, for example, the pharmaceutical industry and the way it prices new drugs, or incrementally improved versions of known drugs, beyond the range of vast numbers of people who need them? That is a great worldwide scandal, with anti-AIDS medicines, for example.

B. Oh, there may well be room, even great room, for improvement. Despite your gibes, I don't think everything is always for the best. I want reform and modification; but not the abolition of the capitalist system to which we owe so much.

A. Take this recent case which shows just what the rule of profit means for medicine. In August 2015, the US businessman Martin Shkreli bought the rights on an old drug called Daraprim, necessary to treat a parasitic infection that can kill people with HIV or cancer. He raised the price of the drug from $13.50 per tablet to $750. That was more shameless than bigger drug companies think they can get away with. Shkreli said he would lower the price. But then he changed his mind, and told a business conference that he would have raised the price higher if given the chance. "My shareholders expect me to make the most profit," he said. "That's the ugly, dirty truth." Indeed! Shkreli is just more shameless, more flamboyant, less cautious than the other drug-extortionists.

B. But Shkreli was arrested for securities fraud in December 2015!

A. Not for raising the price of the drug and pricing sick people out of being able to use it! He was arrested for breaking some financial rules, not for being the living spirit of predatory capitalism in medicine. It's like the murderer Al Capone being jailed for tax evasion. Doesn't it even occur to you that someone capable of what Shkreli did is morally and mentally ill — a sociopath if not a full blown psychopath? He epitomises the capitalist system at its most dehumanised: the psycho-pathology of capitalism.

B. One extreme case proves nothing.

A. It is not just one case. In November 2017 a British government agency denounced a Canadian company for arbitrarily having raised its average price per pack for pills used to control the common condition of hypothyroidism from £4.46 to £258.19, while its production costs remained "broadly stable". In December 2016 the NHS managed to get a US corporation fined for raising the price of a pack of phenytoin sodium pills, taken to control epilepsy, from £2.83 to £67.50. And those two cases are about "generic" drugs, with no patent protection. Drugs are priced as high as the corporations can get away with. Sick people and the NHS are held to ransom, or allowed to die when they could be saved. Even institutions like the NHS find some drugs beyond their capacity to pay for.

The "reward" goes to the shareholders and the top executives of companies like Roche. Those companies institutionalise "science" and "research". They put highly qualified technicians to work in certain areas. They direct collective scientific research, and decide how and where it may or may not be published. All inventions or improvements are their property. What guides their choice of research projects? Potential profitability, not social need, determines what they do, in this field which is so immensely important to all of us. The people being "rewarded" here are not the inventors of drugs that benefit humanity, but a section of the moneyed classes of capitalism. You will remember that not so long ago a company tried to copyright the map of the human genome — to put itself in a position to charge humankind a fee for all the multifarious uses of the new map.

B. As they say in America, they were "only trying to make a buck". You forget the trickle-down benefits of their activities.

A. I saw in a TV program recently that scientists are working on the carcasses of mammoths, tundra-frozen for thousands of years, with the intention of cloning a mammoth. They are financed by a South Korean

CAPITALISM, INVENTORS, AND FUTURE PROGRESS

company, to which their findings will belong by legally airtight contracts. This company already clones pet dogs — at $100,000 a time — for pet-lovers who are both doting and rich.

The vast social networks of science, invention, improvement of old means and methods does not, when you examine it, have much to do with rewarding great discoveries and encouraging others with the prospect of acclaim and wealth. In a sense invention is already "socialised", but for the financial benefit of certain shareholders, and not directly of society.

B. There is some healthy competition between companies. That is better than a state monopoly.

A. Is it? That would depend on who "owned" the state, on the nature of the state in relation to civil society. I repeat: there is no socialist reason why inventors should not get substantial rewards for great work. There is every reason why their inventions should not be turned into capitalist patent-monopoly products.

B. Better that than into state monopolies.

A. Again: I question your premiss. So does history. The people who in the early 1940s developed penicillin for medical use out of Fleming's observations were driven, or mainly driven, by the needs of the British war effort, by the desire to help and heal wounded and sick soldiers. Theirs was part of a social effort, of a broad society-wide feeling of common purpose. Without that, the development of usable medicine from Fleming's observations probably wouldn't have happened for a long time. Here the drive for personal riches and aggrandisement was not central, and certainly not paramount in starting the great antibiotics revolution in medicine. Social need, social effort, social (in this case national) identification was (and very likely hostility to fascism and Nazism too). Why, in the name of common sense, and common decency, do you believe that social responsibility, and the desire to benefit society, would not be a sufficient spur to effort and invention in the future?

B. Experience. Look around you! Look at the precedent of the old Stalinist states!

A. In the last reduction, your picture of the individual being driven only by the prospect of being able to tax other human beings for the use of an invention on which their lives may depend is the stupid idea of human beings as only predatory animals. Of a society in which, in the words of Bartolomeo Vanzetti to the court that sentenced him, and his comrade Sacco, to be burned alive in the electric chair, as they duly were

— "man is wolf to the man".

B. The facts don't lie.

A. Yes they do — especially through the mouths of fools interpreting them in a certain way. You, for instance!

B. There's no foolishness in facing reality.

"Never again war": poster by Käthe Kollwitz, 1924

Is There an Ecological Imperative for Socialism?

A. We live in the age of a "Great Fear", the fear that humankind has irreversibly fouled its ecological nest. There have been other "Great Fears" in the past. For decades it seemed that a series of world wars, or then that nuclear war, would wreck civilisation and open a new regressive dark age. At his death Trotsky was oppressed by the idea that because of the defeats and betrayals of the working-class movement's attempts to replace capitalism with socialism in the previous quarter-century, humankind faced a series of world wars that would be "the grave of civilisation".

B. A bizarre, esoteric idea, surely: personal despair...

A. Not so. If it was personal despair, then many others shared that despair. At the end of the 1930s it was a commonplace fear and expectation. You'll find variants of it in a 1942 Papal Encyclical, in the historian E H Carr's editorials in *The Times*, even in the poetry and journalism of W B Yeats. So, not a case of "they are all out of step except Trotsky".

B. I find that hard to believe.

A. Like many of the other Great Fears of History, it was eclipsed by subsequent events. For many, including eventually the important American socialist, Max Shachtman, it developed into a paralysing fear of world Stalinism, seen as an encroaching barbarism likely to overwhelm both capitalism and the prospect of working-class socialism. The terrified horror with which so many people viewed the H Bomb in the 1950s and 60s was another Great Fear. That subsided with the test ban treaties of the early 1960s, and after the Cuban missile crisis, during which we lived for ten days with the near-certainty that nuclear war was about to start.

B. Well, the groundless fear of ecological ruination of the planet will pass, too. We will muddle through.

A. Groundless? No! The justified, necessary and healthy fear of ecological ruination and social regression as a consequence faces us with stark urgency. There is a serious possibility that capitalism, which first opened up the socialist "option" in history, shifted it from wishful aspiration to practical possibility, will close it again by way of doing irreparable damage to the ecological system on which humankind depends. We cannot know, but there may be limited time in which to mount a socialist society, a fully democratic society, resting on the best achievements of capitalism. I repeat: it may be an option that is foreclosing on us. We cannot afford to be smug.

B. I'm not being smug! I'm refusing to follow you and the others into ecological panic and "the world may end soon" hysteria. Is it even proven that global warming is due to human activity?

A. The expert evidence is that it is. Much of the "debate" about that is a case of people with vested interests and their bought and paid for hired "scientists" muddying the streams of debate.

B. But it isn't certain. Things will turn out all right.

A. We cannot afford to be smugly optimistic about it. What if you are wrong? Inactivity now will (or, to go some of your road with you, may) mean losing the chance to do something about it while there is still time. The reorganisation of the labour movement on a socialist basis is very urgent, because the task of confronting capitalism with a viable socialist alternative is very urgent, and getting more urgent.

B. Alarmism never did anybody any good. It's part of your utopian mindset. Only here it turns into a terrified dystopianism.

A. Contrast the unbelievably laid back and irresponsible way governments are responding to the prospect of irreversible ecological catastrophe with what they did in World War One and World War Two. Then, capitalist governments, faced with fighting major wars, took great powers of direction and control over industry. Britain and the USA were typical examples. Production had to be of whatever the war effort required. The allocation of resources, including labour-power, was subordinated to the governments' perceptions of what would promote or disrupt the waging of war. To a degree that is surprising, looked at from within the dominant ideology of our "new enlightenment", governments took control of the economy into their own hands. They had gone through the 1930s unable to eradicate unemployment, unable or unwilling to control economic forces. Now, when it was a matter of life or state-death, they did it wholeheartedly.

B. It was not socialism!

A. Of course it was not socialism. In both Britain and the USA, and also in Germany, it was a system of war state-capitalism. The capitalists kept their ownership, and made greatly enhanced profits out of the wars. But they operated under government control and direction. "Needs must when the devil drives". Now humankind is faced with the need to fight a new war, a prolonged and prodigious war, to avert a catastrophe immensely greater even than defeat in war would bring, greater even than was brought down upon the great loser in both wars, Germany.

It is a world-wide war to save, preserve, and as far as possible restore the ecological system on which human life and civilisation depends. Increasing numbers of people are becoming aware of that fact. Plainly we need a world economy that doesn't randomly cut down rain-forests for profit, or allow private interests to pollute the atmosphere, or loot irreplaceable resources, or measure things only in terms of profit for the exploiting class, without regard to ecological cost or ultimate human cost.

B. Jesus! Mel Gibson! Mad Max — the socialist! An ecological imperative for socialism? That's just a piece of opportunist special pleading by socialists who as socialists are proven political and ideological bankrupts.

A. The need for a planned economy has been central to socialism for many decades before we — socialists, and people in general — reached our present ecological awareness. That adds extra urgency to it. The economy of the world needs to be planned, brought under rational human control, freed from the tyranny of a market which is blind to human need and blind to the needs of the ecological system on which we depend. And only the working class can do that.

B. There are better answers to the problem than old socialism pinned as an extra tail to the ecological donkey!

A. What are the alternative answers? The urgent task is to find a full and adequate answer to the looming ecological catastrophe towards which the capitalists…

B. Capitalists! The Stalinist systems were the worst polluters and the most wasteful industrialisers. Think of Chernobyl!

A. Indeed, think of Chernobyl. But you interrupted me: ... the ecological catastrophe towards which the capitalists and Stalinists have brought humankind. Little bits of tinkering simply won't do the job. Only rational, overall, world-wide planning according to the real costs of economic processes, including the ecological costs, will answer to the urgent need. Rational planning is by definition democratic planning on every level all through the economy.

B. Let me see if I understand you correctly. You want the governments to impose state controls on the economy such as they had in the World Wars?

A. No. I used that experience to illustrate what could be done when the rulers felt an urgent need, on pain of military defeat. It is a shocking contrast to the lackadaisical approach now to a far, far greater threat. I advocate a planned economy under democratic control. I mean by that workers' control in the industries as well as on the level of government, and democratic planning. The tiny minority of people who own our giganticist economic system must not be allowed to hold humankind to ransom or lead it by the nose to self-destruction. That is what they do now.

B. You want the government to confiscate their property?

A. Not "the government". A socialist workers' government. Small shareholders should be pensioned off — but essentially, yes, big businesses should be expropriated. They themselves live by expropriating the value produced by the working class. The de-nationalisations in Britain under Thatcher were the biggest looting of public property since the common lands were enclosed and stolen, from the 16th century to the 18th. The expropriators will be expropriated, as Karl Marx memorably put it.

B. For the sake of argument I'll accept your definition of the problem. Why not the wartime system you described?

A. A short answer is that it would not meet the scale and likely duration of the problem. And why leave proven incompetents — venal, self-serving, larcenous incompetents — in control and ownership in industry? The wartime arrangements were stop-gap short-term things by governments loyal to the capitalists. What we need is long-term planning, and not the sort of company-wide planning corporations have now, which is steered by the private interests of the owners. We need to eliminate profit-chasing as a consideration in economic and social activity. We need to eliminate the bourgeoisie and their system.

B. God, you're absurd! Trade unions and trade-unionists are among the most bone-headed conservatives. They are the worst "know-nothing" and "Luddite" defenders of vested interests in industry and politics. Any hope for doing something to overcome the ecological problem lies with enlightened employers and the governments they influence, most likely in the teeth of trade-union opposition.

A. And a great job those enlightened capitalists are making of it! Any solution to the ecological crisis adequate in scale and depth to the size of the problem has to be a society-wide and international solution. The big capitalists are not going to do that. It is in absolute antagonism to the necessary modes of capitalist functioning — private ownership, competition, private interests of the capitalist owners in first place. At best they will tinker with it, fumbling and stumbling. Theirs is a world of corporate competition in which the loss of advantage in one country or sector is taken advantage of by competitors, and for that reason feared and shunned. Socialist ideas of society-wide transformation, by the suppression of crude capitalist economic advantage and profiteering, are the only ideas which can clear the way for action on the scale which the crisis demands.

B. You are saying that nothing can be done until the world is transformed by a socialist force which now exists only on a tiny scale — that is, for big politics, does not exist at all. Lobbying and pressure now are at least real things.

A. Lobbying and pressure may do some good. I am not counterposing an ultimate solution to that. As the forces gather for a socialist solution, they will naturally put pressure on the powers that exist. They will massively increase the power and influence of lobbying. But no other class than the working class can break the market-profit nexus and replace it with something better, namely an economy run by human reason, to satisfy human need and bring sustainable human betterment, rather than by the market and the profit interests of the owners of capital. An economy that will put an end to the production of shoddy, short-lived goods with profitable built-in obsolescence, to the tremendous waste of the present system.

William Morris, a pioneer of the Marxist movement in Britain

Poster appealing to German workers to join the young Communist Party (Spartacus League) in 1919, and featuring the martyred Spartacus leader Karl Liebknecht

The "Bird In The Hand"

B. But why should I want socialism? Capitalism has, despite the terrible events of the 20th century — and I'm not denying them — learned a great deal. We have been through a tremendous cycle of capitalist boom and expansion. Things have been getting better, progressively, for a lot of people, for a sizeable portion of humankind, over decades.

And why should I want a social levelling-down, to a grey social uniformity and conformity?

A. Your "grey and uniform" "barracks socialism" is a hostile myth. People with the basics of life secured — food, shelter, health, education — and relieved of the burden of toiling daily for the profits and to the orders of the exploiters, will blossom individually in a way that capitalism makes impossible for most people, most of the time.

B. Why should I pretend that people as people are equal, when they are not equal in capacity, propensity, development and potential for development, achievement and possible achievement? The faults of capitalism, which I don't deny, and in honesty could not deny, are a necessary and therefore worthwhile price to pay for a society that creates wealth, unleashes and encourages personal initiative in all fields. It encourages social mobility, and allows easy entry into its elite ruling class.

A. That's the advertising-agency patter!

B. It exists and can be improved on.

A. "Social mobility" is actually declining, in Britain and in the USA. The children of the working class, and especially of the worst-off sections of the working class, are locked in by the disadvantages which they suffer in their early years. "Social mobility" exists in the ideology of plutocratic society. Its main function is to promote mass social consent for capitalism. You are rather like the man who worshipped a goose strutting around the farmyard in the hope that one day she would lay a great big golden egg, with his name on it.

B. Capitalism does lay golden eggs for quite a few people, you know.

A. The addled fantasy of many people, the passive hope or rather fantasy that one day they will be rich themselves, is a major force in securing general consent for capitalism. It is the same psychology as waiting to win the lottery — and even less probable. The truth is that even limited upward mobility — forget about the dream of sudden riches — is beyond the reach of most people.

B. Even so, some people do move upwards. Some get rich. Look at Bill Gates and the other internet billionaires.

A. In recent decades, in Britain, the child of a higher professional or managerial father has been twenty times more likely to end up in such a high-status job than a child with a working-class father. The Government's Social Mobility Commission found just 5% of children eligible for free school meals gaining 5 A grades at GCSE. In some law firms around 40% of staff were educated at fee-paying or selective schools, and as many as 70% in some elite accountancy firms – compared to 7% in the whole population. Overall, in Britain men's income is 55% correlated with their parents', a higher correlation even than in the USA.

B. Capitalism promotes a thriving market in ideas, it offers choices, it fosters and rewards a free press. Most of the time now, it promotes rational, democratic, and peaceful relations between states. It promotes political democracy. It nurtures rationality and realistic thinking...

A. Like the bungling bankers of 2007-8?

B. There are always exceptions. The bird in my hand is worth a lot to me, more than the birds in the bush and the fields and the skies, no matter how enticing their plumage looks from a distance. The ideal here is the enemy of the possible and improvable. The imagined perfection is the enemy of bit-by-bit achievable improvement. You sacrifice that step-by-step improvement in pursuit of some ideal big-bang replacement that doesn't exist, is yet to be won, and may never be won. And you may bring down upon us stark ruination. Isn't that what the history of the 20th century teaches us?

A. What it teaches smug fainthearts like you! We can make things a lot better than they are now. And, to put it in a nutshell, because we can, we should.

B. Yes, but the fact that you can think something up, and vividly envisage it in your head, doesn't necessarily mean that you can achieve it in reality. The unicorn is created in our imagination by combining characteristics of different animals, just as the creatures in the Star Wars films are. There are no unicorns in reality.

A. No, but in fact, in today's state of knowledge and techniques of biological modifications, we could, I guess, now — or soon — create real unicorns! Dolly the sheep could be Dolly the unicorn.

B. Idiot! Cloning assumes that a unicorn already exists.

A. Genetic modification doesn't... In fact, of course, all domesticated animals, from the poor dumb sheep to the vast range of types of dog, have been created over centuries by human intervention and selective breeding. Existing species are to a great extent the product of all-creative humankind. You sell us short with your fear to contemplate the creation of a society better than capitalism.

B. There — listen to yourself! Now you are fantasising about creating unicorns!

A. No. I'm pointing out that even when you invoke that polemical cliché, even then you lag behind the real social and biological possibilities of the world you live in.

B. Unicorn socialism! Not a bad name for your politics...

A. Your picture of capitalist reality and of history is, to understate it, too one-sided. You attribute to "capitalism" and to the bourgeoisie things which the working class and the plebeians won against the bourgeoisie — the existing democracy is one example. It was won by plebeian struggle, but, along the way, progressively emptied of much of its old meaning by the entrenched ruling classes and their servants and tools. You assume that the desirable things and traits you list are inseparable from capitalism and cannot exist without the present arrangements of society. You assume that under capitalism the gains will continue to exist indefinitely, and go on improving. They will not regress as Europe regressed from progress, and belief in inevitable continuous progress, to Hitler's world, where the medieval ghetto for Jews reappeared in the cities of Europe, and factories were erected for killing human beings and disposing of their bodies.

Socialists believe that the social and human gains won under capitalism can survive capitalism, and that they can develop much more fully once the limits imposed on them by capitalism and private ownership of the economic bases of society are broken.

B. You *believe*, but there is no rational basis for your belief.

A. I think I've shown that there is. But you — you are ridiculously complacent. There were people making the same sort of conservative defence of the then status quo back in the old Stone Age! "If we get too reliant on this new-fangled craze for more refined flint tools, may we not lose what we have thought sufficient for tens of thousands of years?" "Iron? Ugly and foul-coloured stuff. Think of the beauties of bronze, and the artistry with which the bronze forgers lift up all of society!" "Produce with steam power? Dirt, pollution, ruin lies that way — better stick to the handicraft manufactures we have!" "Democracy? How can the many-headed ignorant mass match the wisdom and learning and concentrated enlightenment, the best knitted to the best, as someone said, passed on from father to son through ages, of a good king enhanced in his personal rule by absolute power? Power to do good for his loyal people".

The things you praise were in their time opposed by people like you with similar arguments. "Remake society according to reason, champion what is rational and scrap what isn't? Don't be ridiculous! Tradition! Age-old tradition, the way our parents and great-grandparents and all our ancestors did things — that is the sure road of safety and of preventing society falling under a dictator like Cromwell or Napoleon Bonaparte". No socialist who knows history, and certainly no Marxist, will deny the great achievements of capitalism. Read what the Communist Manifesto said of that. The very possibility of socialism is created by capitalism as it develops the social productivity and social intermeshing of labour.

But today capitalism blocks the further logical development even of the good things it created in history, or allowed the people to create within it. And social regression is possible; if we don't avoid the ecological catastrophes that are a real and immediate threat to our societies, it is inevitable. Think back to the all-suffusing optimism, the confidence in steady improvement, in Europe and America before 1914, and what followed: war, the great slump, Hitler, and a second world war that killed 60 million people and brought physical ruination to large parts of Europe. Germany experienced worse than the devastation in the Thirty Years War in the 17th century.

B. What about the social catastrophes brought by socialism?

A. By Stalinism! But by capitalism, too. Much of capitalist progress is thin, thinner than it need be with the material possibilities of today. Take personal initiative, for instance. Most people are locked into economic and social situations that warp and mutilate them, stifle their development, and snuff out individuality.

B. But we have freedom of the press. And choice.

A. In practice "freedom of the press" for the mass media becomes freedom for newspaper and TV channel owners, like Rupert Murdoch. "Choice" is double-talk. Mostly it means choice, and wide choice, for the well-off. It is a thin ideological garment for the freedom of the moneyed behind which hides the cutting-off for most people of choice about most things, most of the time, including jobs, that is, about how they spend the main part of their entire lives. "For more choice you must have less choice for the rich", as Orwell or some other honest observer might have put it. Above all, the system corrupts humankind and keeps us at the level of predatory animals looking for the chance to rob each other.

The wise scientist Albert Einstein, who was a socialist, summed it up like this: "This crippling of individuals I consider the worst evil of capitalism... An exaggerated competitive attitude is inculcated... [we are] trained to worship acquisitive success... I am convinced there is only one way to eliminate these grave evils, namely through the establishment of a socialist economy, accompanied by an educational system which would be oriented toward social goals".

B. I'd listen to him about physics, but not on social organisation. What did he know?

A. He knew what was wrong with the world he lived in and saw around him. The fundamental argument is that the whole capitalist system is crying out for change — for economic democracy, if you want to put it like that. It is devouring what you say are its great positive achievements. The growth of the multinational corporations undermines the very possibility of the democratic elected governments of most individual states controlling and regulating them.

B. You socialists are rather like the man who killed the gold-laying goose to get all its eggs at once. You don't understand how things work. The golden eggs only evolve, come into existence, in a certain way. Capitalism, the market, economic freedom

A. Mainly for the rich...

B. ... are tremendously productive forces. Look at the riches of the capitalist world which they have produced.

A. Not for everyone, not by a long way! In the USA, lower-income real wages have risen barely, if they have risen at all, since the 1970s. In the UK, median real wages fell 10% between 2008 and 2015, and are still (in 2018) lower than in 2006. The top 10% of households in Britain hold 44% of household wealth, on the latest figures. That inequality is increasing.

B. The period since 2007-8 is an exception, and the USA is an exception. Over the whole history of industrial capitalism, working-class living standards have risen a lot.

A. I'd be the last to deny that working-class organisation and trade-union struggle can win gains under capitalism, have won gains, and will again win gains. Karl Marx, in his time, argued against the idea held by other socialists that working-class living standards were bound to be kept down to an absolute minimum by an "iron law of wages" which no working-class action could change. But he argued that capitalism has an organic tendency to increase inequality and insecurity for the working class. He was right.

Look at the cost in human terms of the system and its selectively bestowed bounties. Look at the world slump since 2007-8 and its tremendous human costs, all due to greed-mad bankers who ran the financial system on which so much in society depends for their private enrichment — for their own and shareholders' benefit. Look what results in the health service when profits and competition are introduced: the destruction of activities which are socially necessary even though economically unprofitable. That is true everywhere when private profit rules and regulates.

B. Yes, there are problems, social and ecological costs, if you want to dwell on that sort of thing, and of course socialists do. Even so, private profit, the drive for private enrichment, is the dynamo at the heart of what our society has produced. You would destroy that mainspring.

A. Ah, the Good, the Blessed, the all-shaping, law-giving, Divine Eternal Market!

B. I repeat: your objection to it is a form of kitsch-Christian morality, economically and socially ignorant. The harsh, or if you like, the sad, truth is that, as the man said, "Greed is good". It's not "nice", but it's good. That's the truth. Get used to it. Live with it, because it rules the world you live in, and always will.

A. Certainly, socialists want to live in a world governed by human solidarity — immediately, that means working-class solidarity — and not by the morality derived from brute-raw nature in which society is a jungle and everyone is a real or just-waiting-for-the-chance predator on everyone else. Where the big, successful predators rule. As Albert Einstein put it, we see today "a community the members of which are unceasingly striving to deprive each other of the fruits of their collective labour", and we socialists will change that.

B. So you hope! But it's plain that you are not at all certain you'll win.

And What's In It For Me?

B. Why waste your life on this foolish quest? Why invite me to do the same? Why fight for a cause that may suffer nothing but defeat, in your lifetime, or forever?

A. Because people should fight for what they know is right, is best, is necessary. They should take responsibility for the fate of society and of humanity. The liberation of humankind from class society, and immediately of the working class within that society from wage-slavery, is, as someone said, the greatest cause in the world. That has been said often. It remains a fundamental truth to guide honest and responsible people.

B. Fools like you!

A. Yes, all the socialists in history were, like me, mere fools compared to your all-wise and very smug self... There are in the history of our movement people who could not and can not be bought, bullied, intimidated, brainwashed or demoralised into serving the rulers or into giving up on the hope of anything better. Rosa Luxemburg, and her comrades Karl Liebknecht and Leo Jogiches, who were murdered too, are good examples of those; and there have been immense numbers of them whose names we don't know, who didn't leave a written legacy. But they left a legacy all right. They augmented, gave life to, nurtured, sustained in their time, and passed on the tradition of working-class socialist revolt and its written legacy from such as Rosa Luxemburg.

B. A big, lovely bunch of losers!

A. Luxemburg and Liebknecht and their comrades, who stood out against the monstrous First World War, were the best people in their generation. They left us a great example and a great and enduring social and political legacy. They augmented the immediate battles of the workers, and fed life to the tradition and the culture of working people and working-class revolt. They nurtured and sustained it and passed it on.

B. Myths to comfort yourself with! Even supposing I were to agree with you so far, what's in it for me? Why should I bother? Why spend even a small part of my life, waste even an instant of my too-short sentience, on advocating socialism? If it is as socially, historically, and morally necessary as you say it is, if the activity of the monopoly capitalists themselves works in favour of the "invading socialist society" — why, then it will inevitably break through without my help. And if it needs my help, then by implication I have no guarantee that we will succeed, so I'd most likely be wasting my life on something hopeless. There is nothing that you or I or the little band of addled zealots to which you belong can do to affect events. The lesson of the 20th century here is that socialism is hopeless, and that your Marxist brand of socialism is doubly hopeless because of its absurd attachment to the daft idea that the working class and only the working class can bring it about.

A. Is it? There is a great deal that we can do here and now, and in some cases what a socialist organisation does can shape large events.

B. How can what you do now impact on the great structural realities of the world?

A. Here and now socialists immerse themselves in the working-class struggles going on around us, whether large-scale or small-scale. Often we make a big difference. And we join in single-issue campaigns, making the links with socialist goals and perspectives. We make a difference there, too.

B. But all that is incremental change within capitalism. How can it have any effect of changing the whole system? You will be defeated.

A. The working class and the socialists may be defeated. If I offered you "guarantees" of victory, I would be a fool! There is only one thing we can guarantee: if we are beaten, we will rise again. And again. And again. That is what history teaches. What can we, the socialists, do? How can what we do — educational work, essentially — reshape the world? We work by patient explanation and discussion of our common social reality to convince the working class of the truth of what we say about capitalism. To see its real wage-slave place in capitalist society, and capitalism's place in history, as one of a number of exploitative class societies. We work to help the working class to become, in political and social affairs, a "class for itself". To see itself as the protagonist of contemporary history. To want to shape and reshape history.

B. You work to brainwash and mislead workers!

A. We work to enlighten and educate them, to help free their minds of the capitalist-serving ideas imposed on society as its ruling ideas by the ruling class and its propagandists.

B. To confuse, mislead, and corrupt intellectually, you mean!

A. To explain to working-class people the realities of a wage-slave society, on the basis of their own experience. A socialist organisation is irreplaceably a body that educates the working class, that helps workers emancipate themselves from the ruling-class miseducation in which they are immersed.

B. Nonsense! I don't recognise that picture of reality.

A. Have you looked in a mirror lately? There is a radical contradiction in the heads of working-class people between the ideas about themselves, about society and their place in it, about history and about capitalism, and their own experience and interests. Workers can and do, at times, make great jumps ahead ideologically. The contradiction catapults them forward. Thus in history we have repeatedly seen tremendous progress towards socialist ideas in short periods. A socialist organisation which starts off small can be decisive in preparing, promoting, clarifying, and consolidating that progress. In our ideas, the ideas we spread among the working class, we bear the seeds of such transformations.

B. A socialist organisation doesn't just act as an educational agency, in which capacity it may be harmless though ineffectual. It agitates, causes strikes, riots, conflicts with the police. Sometimes it misguides workers into armed insurrection. Look at what the bloody Bolsheviks did in 1917!

A. Socialist organisations do all those things. In history socialists have done all that, and more. We will do that in future. But everything we can do, or aspire to do, in that respect, depends at any given moment on the thinking of the working class. It is the workers who act, even if they are led by socialists. Everything a socialist organisation does, up to organising insurrections, is conditioned by its first duty and its primary activity: to help the working class free itself from ideas such as yours. Even a small group of socialists can do tremendous work in the battle of ideas.

B. I asked what's in it for me, and you answer with a soliloquy on a "struggle" which you and yours have been pursuing, but in which you concede that you may not succeed — that you may be crushed.

A. When you are part of a collective, then narrow "self-interest" is often in the longer term shown to have been not in anybody's interest at all. Here we need to go beyond mere political considerations into such questions as what life is all about — what should a life be about? We go into the world of personal ethical considerations, options, and responsibilities.

B. Ah, philosophy! Morality again. Monty Python-Trotsky and the Meaning of Life!

A. Are we nothing higher than a commercially-conducted and regulated edition of animals, amongst them primitive humankind, spending an entire lifetime browsing and grubbing for food? That is the "shop until you drop" ethos which this society glorifies and depends on for economic dynamism. Leavened maybe with a bit of religious uplift, a half-tongue-in-cheek consultation with a horoscope to see what "the stars" are going to do to you? Maybe the small and tame bacchanalia of a pop festival once a year or so?

If you are a worker, are you content to spend most of your life doing work you don't care about — or do care about, but are forced to do in a way you can't find fulfilling — for an employer whose only concern is to coin profit out of you and the work you do? Will you settle into being a docile wage-slave, breeding and rearing children to be the next generation of wage-slaves?

Or will you rebel? Will you be content with the story the bourgeoisie and their media tell of themselves, and of you, or will you inquire for yourself, and study the literature of the rebels against capitalism, the Marxists? Will you join the labour movement, help build it up, fight for it against the masters of capitalist society?

If you are a student, what are you going to do when you leave university? If you are a one-time left-wing student, now working, what do you do?

Of course, you have to live, and you live in this society, not in the sort of society you might choose. You will have to get a job. If not an ideal one, you may still get a better job than you would have without your studies. Maybe one where (as some people say) you "love your work but hate your job". But can you, should you, put your best energies into "making a career"?

Will you teach? In a school in a low-income area, where you will participate in the heart-breaking reality of kids going through school and emerging semi-literate? When you know that only changes in society, not just the efforts of individual teachers, will change that? And where you will have to use more energy on complying with the box-ticking, exam-obsessed, impositions of school management and exam boards than on responding to the needs of your pupils?

Will you become a university teacher, retailing second and third hand opinion and received capitalist wisdom, with a bit of academic-Marxist criticism, perhaps, for leaven and for the sake of your conscience? If you get an academic job with more scope, will you be a left-wing academic consumer of "revolutionary" anti-capitalist theory, but not do anything about it in practice by spreading understanding to the people at large, specifically to the working class, and helping them organise to fight for it?

Will you be a nurse? A doctor? You'll see the heartbreak of a National

Health Service in chaos, with desperately needed medical care "rationed" by way of waiting times and increasingly by markets, and the enormous and crippling amounts of money paid out to the pharmaceutical companies. Will you become a chemist working for a pharmaceutical company? You might help invent a great medical step forward — and see it used as an expensive commodity, available only to those who can pay or have the welfare state pay, in order to make profit for the bosses and shareholders of the company.

Will you go to a poorer country and make life a little better for people who, in a rich and supposedly civilised world, are dying for lack of money to buy food and even comparatively cheap medicines? Will you be a social worker? You will be providing inadequate help to the victims of poverty, poor education, unemployment, and migration far from home. At best you'll help them organise their lives a bit better, with inadequate means and devastatingly arid prospects.

Will you be an immigration official? Help regiment migrant workers and their families; sort out the "legals" from the "illegals"; be part of a system which demonises, hunts down, imprisons, and deports the "illegals"?

Be a journalist? You won't be a privileged columnist, with some right to express a personal opinion (within the limits regulated by the choice of the newspaper and TV owners who can grant you that privilege). There are very few such jobs. As a run-of-the-mill newspaper or TV journalist, you can't help but contribute in some degree to the selection, slanting, and "balancing" of the millionaire-owned opinion-forming machine in which you will be a voice in a chorus singing what the others sing, what you are told to sing from the bourgeois hymn-book.

You can't help but participate in a biased selection of what is "newsworthy", in presenting capitalism and "all its works and pomps" as something immutable and fixed; in suppressing discussion of the socialist alternatives that the crisis of capitalism has given a relevance which they seemed not to have in the days of the long capitalist boom before 2007-8.

Will you become a professional politician? Go from school and university, perhaps through office in a student union, on to be a "researcher" and maybe then a parliamentary candidate? That is, mould and shape yourself to fit into the political machinery that runs the system? The modern mainstream politician is a rancid mix of actor, reciting prescribed lines, and lawyer, arguing a brief from whichever side of the issue is indicated, without real conviction or real concern for what is true or best for society.

Will you become a trade-union official? You will be in the labour movement, but "professionally" barred from being able to tell workers openly what you think about the issues that arise and about the union leadership and its policies. Will you limit yourself to helping workers get a little more wages in the labour market — some of the time! — but also inadvertently helping the union machinery and the top leaders regiment and limit working-class responses to their own exploitation, bamboozlement and degradation?

Will you become a civil servant and keep your head down? Become some other sort of official, functioning as a cog in a bureaucratic machine, serving capitalism?

You have to get a job. But to put your best energies into any of those jobs, or similar ones, is self-serving in the narrowest financial and consumerist sense. It would be, for you, self-submerging and self-destroying in the sense of destroying your critical overview of what is right and wrong. It would, I put it to you, be deeply irresponsible.

Most students — most rebellious students too — go on as they get older to excise parts of themselves so that they can fit in to a career like those I've just surveyed. Don't you think that we socialist militants have a better idea? You have to live in society as it is, but you don't have to fool yourself and, as you get older, mutilate and repudiate your better, younger self. You don't have to prostitute yourself.

You can be better than that. You are better than that! You can be an enemy of capitalism and of its political machine and its opinion-industries. You can study the Marxist critique of capitalism — and maybe develop it — and be active, in your workplace, in your everyday life, on the streets, to prepare the working class to rise and make a better society, a far better society, one free from the evils that make capitalism an abomination, and all the more abominable because something better is possible now.

Individual life should not be clad in narrowly personal and familial asbestos-skinned egotism — "I'm all right, Jack, fuck the others" — conscience-salved perhaps with a donation here and there to charitable institutions such as War on Want or Oxfam. Anyway, "society" may not leave you alone. An awful lot of people hypnotised by the values of commercialism have had to wake up from that sleep to the fact that they have been like the legendary St Brendan, the Dark-Ages Irish monk who made his camp on a solid island in the sea, lit his fire to cook, and found it moving under him: it wasn't an island, it was a whale.

I put it to you that a better philosophy of life than the prevailing one is to face the fact that we are, each of us, part of a broader social entity, and that we should concern ourselves with its well-being as a necessary way of securing our own and our children's and grandchildren's well-being. I recently came across the following words, said to a journalist by the actress Marilyn Monroe, a woman of the left who had had to fight her way through the sewers of capitalist society.

She summed up much of what socialists seek in simple words that might have come from William Morris: "What I really want to say is that what the world really needs is a real feeling of kinship. Everybody, stars, labourers, Negroes, Jews, Arabs: we are all brothers. Please don't make me a joke. End the interview with what I believe".

We should concern ourselves with the moral climate around us, if only in the interests of our children and their children, and do something to counter the mind-rotting morality bred in us by capitalism and reinforced by it. The morality for which, as someone well said, everything has a price but nothing an intrinsic or transcendent value. We should not peacefully exist in and with a society in which the precondition for workers to live is that they submit to being wage slaves, and accept that their productive energies are owned and controlled by employers who take a large part of the new wealth the workers create.

We should not settle into accepting fatalistically that a large part of humanity, including many in whose midst we live, suffer in hunger, ignorance, and needless disease. We should not live without trying to do something about the slaughter of millions of children in worse-off countries on the altar of capitalist necessity. We should not be passive consumers only, but also try to create something better, or contribute to its creation.

All that aside, the root argument why you should join us is that you know that humankind under capitalism lives in a world of savage exploitations, inequalities, and profound injustice. Needless, shameful, damnable injustice. At stake here is the future of democracy, of equality, of all that is good in the society humankind has so far created, and of humankind itself. Have the courage to hope and to fight to realise your best hopes and desires. Slough off and break your paralysing sense of irony, unworthiness, absurdity, and, as James Connolly used to put it, *dare to hope and dare to fight*. Entrench yourself in the attitude expressed by one of Connolly's comrades of the 1916 Rising:

"Did ye think to conquer the people,
Or that law is stronger than life,
And than our desire to be free?
We will try it out with you,
Ye that have harried and held,
Ye that have bullied and bribed.
Tyrants… hypocrites… liars!"

As the early socialists said: "A full, free, happy life — for all or for none!

Hope, and fight.

A photograph of strikers from the heroic period of the German workers' movement before 1914. The text reads: 22 weeks. Ten-hour day fighters from Crimmitschau. Up with solidarity! 18 January 1904.

Karl Marx; Frederick Engels; the Bolshevik leader Inessa Armand, who died in 1920; Eleanor Marx, daughter of Karl, who was a trade-union activist as well as a socialist.

Posters from France, May 1968. Continue the struggle, capitalism is foundering; Beauty is in the street; Break the old mechanisms; Workers, immigrant, French, all united.

What socialists do, and why we do it

WHAT IS THE SOCIALIST REVOLUTION? How does it relate to the existing system? What makes the socialists' belief in their own cause rational, the product of a scientific view of history, despite the present weakness of socialism?

Capitals grow by the eating up of the smaller by the bigger capitals, in a progression that has led in our time to global companies richer than many governments. Today, world-wide, the capitalist classes are dominant in a way less than ever before alloyed by old customs and compromises, and they are more closely intermeshed across national frontiers. Simultaneously, the old measures of social provision implemented by Western welfare states and Third World bureaucratic regimes are being stripped away. Inequality between rich and poor is increasing worldwide, and within most individual countries.

Marx explained: "Hand in hand with centralisation, or this expropriation of many capitalists by few, develop, on an ever-extending scale, the co-operative form of the labour-process, the conscious technical application of science, the methodical cultivation of the soil, the transformation of the instruments of labour into instruments of labour only usable in common, the economising of all means of production by their use as means of production of combined, socialised labour, the entanglement of all peoples in the net of the world-market, and with this, the international character of the capitalistic regime.

"Along with the constantly diminishing number of the magnates of capital, who usurp and monopolise all advantages of this process of transformation, grows the mass of misery, oppression, slavery, degradation, exploitation; but with this too grows the revolt of the working-class, a class always increasing in numbers, and disciplined, united, organised by the very mechanism of the process of capitalist production itself.

"The monopoly of capital becomes a fetter upon the mode of production, which has sprung up and flourished along with, and under it. Centralisation of the means of production and socialisation of labour at last reach a point where they become incompatible with their capitalist integument. This integument is burst asunder. The knell of capitalist private property sounds. The expropriators are expropriated...

"This does not re-establish private property for the producer, but gives him individual property based on the acquisition of the capitalist era: i.e., on co-operation and the possession in common of the land and of the means of production...

"The transformation of capitalistic private property, already practically resting on socialised production, into socialised property... is the expropriation of a few usurpers by the mass of the people".

The revolutionary potential of the working class

Capitalism rests on the exploitation of wage workers, people with no property in the means of production and only their own labour power to sell — the proletariat. Capitalism creates the proletariat. What do we mean when we say that the proletariat is central to the socialist alternative to capitalism?

Marx again: "The first attempt of workers to associate among themselves always takes place in the form of combinations. Large-scale industry concentrates in one place a crowd of people unknown to one another. Competition divides their interests. But the maintenance of wages, this common interest which they have against their boss, unites them in a common thought of resistance — combination. Thus combination always has a double aim, that of stopping competition among the workers, so that they can carry on general competition with the capitalist.

"If the first aim of resistance was merely the maintenance of wages, combinations, at first isolated, constitute themselves into groups as the capitalists in their turn unite for the purpose of repression, and in the face of always united capital, the maintenance of the association becomes more necessary to them than that of wages. This is so true that English economists are amazed to see the workers sacrifice a good part of their wages in favour of associations, which, in the eyes of these economists, are established solely in favour of wages. In this struggle — a veritable civil war — all the elements necessary for a coming battle unite and develop. Once it has reached this point, association takes on a political character. Economic conditions had first transformed the mass of the people of the country into workers. The combination of capital has created for this mass a common situation, common interests. This mass is thus already a class as against capital, but not yet for itself. In the struggle, of which we have noted only a few phases, this mass becomes united, and constitutes itself as a class for itself. The interests it defends becomes class interests. But the struggle of class against class is a political struggle...

"When it is a question of making a precise study of strikes, combinations and other forms in which the proletarians carry out before our eyes their organisation as a class, some are seized with real fear and others display a transcendental disdain. An oppressed class is the vital condition for every society founded on the antagonism of classes. The emancipation of the oppressed class thus implies necessarily the creation of a new society. For the oppressed class to be able to emancipate itself, it is necessary that the productive powers already acquired and the existing social relations should no longer be capable of existing side by side. Of all the instruments of production, the greatest productive power is the revolutionary class itself. The organisation of revolutionary elements as a class supposes the existence of all the productive forces which could be engendered in the bosom of the old society.

"Does this mean that after the fall of the old society there will be a new class domination? No. The condition for the emancipation of the working class is the abolition of every class, just as the condition for the liberation of the third estate, of the bourgeois order, was the abolition of all estates and all orders. The working class, in the course of its development, will substitute for the old civil society an association which will exclude classes and their antagonism...

"Meanwhile the antagonism between the proletariat and the bourgeoisie is a struggle of class against class, a struggle which carried to its highest expression is a total revolution. Indeed, is it at all surprising that a society founded on the opposition of classes should culminate in brutal contradiction, the shock of body against body, as its final denouement?

"Do not say that social movement excludes political movement. There is never a political movement which is not at the same time social. It is only in an order of things in which there are no more classes and class antagonisms that social evolutions will cease to be political revolutions. Till then, on the eve of every general reshuffling of society, the last word of social science will always be: 'Le combat ou la mort; la lutte sanguinaire ou le néant. C'est ainsi que la question est invinciblement posée.'" [From the novel *Jean Siska* by George Sand: "Combat or Death: bloody struggle or extinction. It is thus that the question is inexorably put".]

Blockages and obstacles

Today the wage-working class is, for the first time in history, probably the largest social class on the planet. There are probably also more organised workers across the world than ever before, with maybe 200 million trade unionists today. Nominal trade union numbers were bigger before 1989, but were artificially inflated by including the members of the state-controlled fake unions of the USSR, Eastern Europe, etc.

But the idea that they exist to replace capitalism with a higher system, to take humankind to socialism, is not the guiding principle of these labour movements. Explosions recur, both in the older capitalist countries and the newer ones. But even when the working class struggles and organises on a large scale, it finds that capitalism has tremendous flexibility for accommodating such struggles and for seducing and pacifying the leaders of workers' organisations.

Earlier generations of socialists thought of the transition from capitalism to socialism as a much more simple business than it has proved to be, as something covering a shorter time span than it is taking. They thought of the self-preparation of the working class to lead humankind out of capitalist neo-barbarism as much more straightforward thing than it has been.

Labour movements experience not only phases of growth and political development, but also phases of destruction and defeat — such as that experienced by the revolutionary labour movement before World War Two — of decay, decline and political regression, and then, again, periods of new growth and political refocusing.

The bourgeoisie too spent ages as a class that needed to remake society in its own image. It took the bourgeoisie, living within feudalism and monarchist absolutist systems, hundreds of years to make itself fit to be the ruling class. It went through many phases, experienced false starts, defeats, was led into "historical compromises" with its class-antagonists.

Yet as a revolutionary class it had immense advantages compared to the proletariat in capitalist society. Its wealth, power, self-rule and historical self-awareness grew even within the old system; the growth of markets, the increasing role of money in the old society, cleared its way and made it socially a subordinate segment of the exploiters even before it ruled. By contrast, the working class in capitalism remains the basic exploited class: it can progress only by independent organisation and by way of its social and political awareness. It can progress only by building a labour and socialist movement.

The Russian labour movement which, led by the Bolshevik Party, took state power in October 1917 was, in the sharpness of its theory and the adequacy of the revolutionary practice guided by that theory, the highest point reached by the working class in world history so far. It remains the great model and guide for the socialists who have come after it.

The activists and the spontaneous struggle

George Plekhanov answered the question "What is the socialist movement"? "Shortly before the revolutionary year of 1848 there emerged among the Socialists men who looked at socialism in a completely new perspective. Seen in this new perspective the principal error of previous Socialists was precisely the fact that [for them] 'future history resolves itself, in their eyes, into propaganda and the practical implementation of their social plans'. The Socialists with the new outlook saw in the future history of the civilised world something else, something incomparably more promising. What precisely did the Socialists with the new outlook see in it? Above all class struggle, the struggle of the exploited with the exploiters, the proletariat with the bourgeoisie. In addition they saw in it the inevitability of the impending triumph of the proletariat, the fall of the present bourgeois social order, the socialist organisation of production and the corresponding alteration in the relationships between people, i.e. even the destruction of classes, among other things.

"Although they knew full well (better than their predecessors) that the socialist revolution involves a complete transformation in all social relationships, the Socialists of the new tendency did not concern themselves at all with working out a plan for the future organisation of society.

"If for the followers of scientific socialism the whole future history of bourgeois society resolves itself in the struggle of the proletariat with the bourgeoisie, all their practical tasks are prompted by precisely this class struggle. Standing resolutely on the side of the proletariat, the new Socialists do everything in their power to facilitate and hasten its victory. But what exactly can they do in this case? A necessary condition for the victory of the proletariat is its recognition of its own position, its relations with its exploiters, its historic role and its socio-political tasks.

"For this reason the new Socialists consider it their principal, perhaps even their only, duty to promote the growth of this consciousness among the proletariat, which for short they call its class consciousness. The whole success of the socialist movement is measured for them in terms of the growth in the class consciousness of the proletariat. Everything that helps this growth they see as useful to their cause: everything that slows it down as harmful. Anything that has no effect one way or the other is of no consequence for them, it is politically uninteresting.

"You will only be recognised as a Socialist if your activity has directly facilitated the growth of the class consciousness of the proletariat. If it does not exert this direct influence then you are not a Socialist at all, even though the more or less remote consequences of your non-socialist activity may bring some degree of advantage for the cause of socialism. My view, I hope, is sufficiently clear. It is expressed in its entirety in the epigram: *Without workers who are conscious of their class interests there can be no socialism.*

"If I assert that the promotion of the growth of the class consciousness of the proletariat is the sole purpose and the direct and sacred duty of the Socialists, then this does not mean that the contemporary Socialists stand for propaganda, for propaganda alone, and for nothing but propaganda. In the broad sense of the word this is perhaps true, but only in the very broad sense. In general it is not easy to draw the line between agitation and what is usually called propaganda. Agitation is also propaganda, but propaganda that takes place in particular circumstances, that is in circumstances in which even those who would not normally pay any attention are forced to listen to the propagandist's words. Propaganda is agitation that is conducted in the normal everyday course of the life of a particular country. Agitation is propaganda occasioned by events that are not entirely ordinary and that provoke a certain upsurge in the public mood. Socialists would be very bad politicians if they were not to use such notable events for their own ends".

Side by side with the broad, elemental class struggle of the working class — and with some autonomy from it, not necessarily on the same rhythms and tempos — a certain proportion of each generation of young people growing up under capitalism become convinced that they must fight to replace this society of exploitation and competition by socialism, a society of solidarity. And some of them are consolidated as activists.

For working-class struggles to move towards revolutionary conclusions, what is needed is that those activists organise themselves; educate themselves; keep their theory and their revolutionary drive bright and sharp; and integrate themselves into the existing labour movement and win respect there, so that at critical moments of class battle they can directly challenge the old time-serving leaders and prevent the diversion of the "spontaneous socialist" impulses of the workers in struggle.

That way the activists can win wider influence, recruit new activists, refresh their own ideas by learning from the battles, and ultimately enlarge, improve, and sharpen their organisation so that at one of the inevitable points where large working-class struggle coincides with drastic internal crisis for capitalism they can lead the working class to revolutionary victory.

That is what the Russian Marxists did between the 1880s and 1917. In Russia the first revolutionary socialists — most of whom also considered themselves "Marxists" — were the populists. The development of the Russian Marxist movement involved a small section of activists separating themselves off from a populist movement which, though in crisis, was still large, active, and influential, in order to argue in theoretical pamphlets for a new approach.

That approach was summed up by Plekhanov in the idea that the Marxists were "convinced that not the workers are necessary for the revolution, but the revolution for the workers"

Later the Marxists became a mass movement in 1905, only to split definitively and be reduced to very small numbers of reliable activists in the years of reaction which followed. As Lenin put it, "Russia achieved Marxism... through the agony she experienced in half a century of unparalleled torment and sacrifice, of unparalleled revolutionary heroism, incredible energy, devoted searching, study, practical trial, disappointment, verification, and comparison with European experience".

The revolutionary party

The working class is unique among all revolutionary classes in that it remains a class of wage slaves until, by seizing political power and the means of production, it makes the decisive step towards emancipating itself. Contrast the classic bourgeois experience.

The bourgeoisie develops historically within feudalism and neo-feudalism as part of a division of labour within society which allows the bourgeoisie to own a segment of the means of production, and itself to be an exploiter, long before it takes political power in society. It thus builds up wealth, culture, systems of ideas to express its interests and view of the world. It, so to speak, ripens organically, and the taking of power, the sloughing off of the old system — even if accompanied by violence — represents the natural maturing and growth of a class already in possession of important means of production and a share of the surplus. The working class remains an exploited class — in more developed capitalist countries, the basic exploited class — up to the death knell of bourgeois social and political rule. It does not accumulate leisure, wealth or its own distinct culture. Its natural condition as a raw social category is to be dominated by the ideas of the ruling class. Its own natural and spontaneous self-defence and bargaining within the capitalist system — trade unionism — binds it ideologically to the ruling class, to bargaining within the system and in times of crisis taking responsibility for it. Its natural tribunes and intellectuals are the trade union bureaucracy.

On the face of it the proletariat might be doomed to go through history as a subordinate class. Marx and Engels themselves wrote: "The ruling ideology in every society is the ideology of the ruling class." In fact the working class becomes a revolutionary class, conscious of its own historic class interests and possibilities in the following way, according to the views of Marx, Engels, Lenin and Trotsky. A set of social theories is created and developed on the basis of bourgeois social science (economics, philosophy, history) which uncovers the necessary logic of the historic evolution of capitalism towards the completion of its organic tendency to become more and more social and monopolistic — by way of common ownership and the abolition of capitalism. The proletariat is located as the protagonist in this stage of history. A segment of the intellectuals of the bourgeoisie comes over to the proletarian wage slaves.

The proletariat itself evolves as a class through the stage of primitive elemental revolt at being driven into the capitalist industrial hell-holes to the stage of organising itself in combinations to get fair wages, and then to the stage of banding itself together for political objectives.

Instead of control of a portion of the means of production, the working class develops its own organisations. Within these organisations a struggle takes place between the ideas that represent the historic interests of the proletariat — Marxism — and the ideas of the bourgeoisie. This struggle occurs even where Marxists are the founders of the labour movement.

Antonio Gramsci summed up the threefold nature of the class struggle: "We know that the proletariat's struggle against capitalism is waged on three fronts: the economic, the political and the ideological. The economic struggle has three phases: resistance to capitalism, i.e. the elementary trade-union phase; the offensive against capitalism for workers' control of production; and the struggle to eliminate capitalism through socialisation.

"The political struggle too has three principal phases: the struggle to check the bourgeoisie's power in the parliamentary State, in other words to maintain or create a democratic situation, of equilibrium between the classes, which allows the proletariat to organise; the struggle to win power and create the workers' State, in other words a complex political activity through which the proletariat mobilises around it all the anti-capitalist social forces (first and foremost the peasant class) and leads them to victory; and the phase of dictatorship of the proletariat, organised as a ruling class to eliminate all the technical and social obstacles which prevent the realisation of communism.

"The economic struggle cannot be separated from the political struggle, nor can either of them be separated from the ideological struggle.

"In its first, trade-union phase, the economic struggle is spontaneous; in other words, it is born inevitably of the very situation in which the proletariat finds itself under the bourgeois order. But in itself, it is not revolutionary; in other words, it does not necessarily lead to the overthrow of capitalism...

"For the trade-union struggle to become a revolutionary factor, it is necessary for the proletariat to accompany it with political struggle: in other words, for the proletariat to be conscious of being the protagonist of a general struggle which touches all the most vital questions of social organisation; i.e. for it to be conscious that it is struggling for socialism...

"The element of consciousness is needed, the 'ideological' element: in other words, an understanding of the conditions of the struggle, the social relations in which the worker lives, the fundamental tendencies at work in the system of those relations, and the process of development which society undergoes as a result of the existence within it of insoluble antagonisms, etc.

"The three fronts of proletarian struggle are reduced to a single one for the party of the working class, which is this precisely because it resumes and represents all the demands of the general struggle. One certainly cannot ask every worker from the masses to be completely aware of the whole complex function which his class is destined to perform in the process of development of humanity. But this must be asked of members of the party. One cannot aim, before the conquest of the State, to change completely the consciousness of the entire working class... But the party can and must, as a whole, represent this higher consciousness."

The blight of Stalinism

For more than 100 years, things other than working class defeat and the continuation of capitalism to this stage have been possible. Working class victory and the beginning of a rational socialist system were possible; but we have had defeats. Trotsky, who had helped the Russian workers in October 1917 demonstrate that the working class suffers from no inbuilt organic political incapacity, understood that the crux of the crisis of human civilisation in the mid-20th century was a crisis of the labour movement. Great labour movements had been created on the perspective of preparing the working class to suppress wage labour and capitalism — a working class that would make itself the ruling class, and freeing itself from capitalism, begin to free humankind from class society. The leaderships, bureaucracies and upper layers of the old socialist movement had, when the first imperialist World War broke out, delivered the labour movements into the hands of their bourgeois enemy as cannon fodder and butchers of the workers of other nations.

The Communist International had been created in 1919 and after to restore independent working class politics after the collapse of 1914. The Stalinist counter-revolution in the USSR in the 1920s tied the Communist International to the new bureaucratic ruling class in the USSR.

When, after 1929, capitalism reached the stage of convulsive semi-collapse, powerful labour movements existed that were strong enough to kick it into its historical grave. But they were everywhere tied to either the bourgeoisie, through the reform-socialist labour movements, or to the Russian ruling class, through its Communist Parties. Trotsky wrote of their "perfidy" and "betrayal".

In the confusion created by the existence of big socialist parties that weren't socialist, and big Communist Parties that weren't communist, the working class suffered murderous accumulating defeat. Trotsky organised the tiny forces that could be organised to compete, with desperate urgency, for the leadership of the working class against the perfidious incumbent leaderships. But Trotsky and everything he represented were defeated and — as we have to recognise in retrospect — defeated for a whole historical period. Capitalism renewed itself on the mass graves, on the destroyed means of production and the ruined cities of the Second World War and began a long period of expansion. Stalinism survived, expanded, and then slowly asphyxiated in its own bureaucratic caul until, in Europe, it collapsed.

Big labour movements grew in Western Europe, especially, in the new Golden Age of capitalism between 1950 and the early 1970s. But they grew deeply imbued with reformism and, often, Stalinist ideas. When they exploded into big battles between 1968 and the early 80s, new revolutionary-minded groupings grew, but not sufficient, and not sufficiently clear, to reconstruct a mass revolutionary socialist culture in the time available.

Defeats in the early 1980s allowed a new, more aggressive, mode of capitalist rule to consolidate, and led to a slow ebbing of the old labour movements. New labour movements emerged in new industrial centres, but, again, not yet revolutionary in temper.

The collapse of the USSR in 1991 came at a time when the workers' movement in the West had been on the retreat for a decade. It fuelled a great surge of capitalist triumphalism, which continues to this day. In many countries it demoralised and dissipated large numbers of the men and women who considered themselves "communists" and "socialists" and who really were the people who provided the activist backbone of the labour movement, the trade union branches and the workplace committees. It created wider openings for the genuine communists, the Trotskyists. But the collapse also revealed how much, in the long years of its isolation, the Trotskyist milieu had become waterlogged with seepage from Stalinism. Today groupings like the SWP, nominally Trotskyist, actually operate more like a small replica of the 1960s Communist Parties, their politics dominated by the "popular front" approach both internationally and in domestic politics.

Who are we, the AWL? We are those who continue to fight for independent working-class politics and for working-class self-liberation against both capitalism and reactionary anti-capitalism (such as Islamic fundamentalism). We are those who continue, as best we can, the Trotskyism of Trotsky and his comrades in the 1930s, rather than extrapolating the cod "orthodox Trotskyism" shaped in the 1940s and early 1950s into a Stalinist-influenced neo-populism. We are the pioneers of the future mass revolutionary workers' parties which will be free of Stalinist seepage and sharp-edged in their drive for independent working-class struggle.

Marxists today

It is impossible to tell how long it will take the working class to make itself ready to suppress capitalism and take humankind forward. It is more easily definable in terms of things that must be accomplished.

The labour movements again need to learn by way of their own experience and by the enlightening work of socialists:
• that capitalism is neither natural nor eternal;

• that it is a historically finite system whose inner processes — the creation and recreation of a proletariat and the relentless socialisation of the means of production, of which "globalisation" is the latest manifestation — prepare its own end;

• that capitalism digs its own grave;

• that the working class, which finds no class in society "lower" than itself and which can only organise the economy collectively, that is, democratically, is the representative within capitalism of the post-capitalist future, and the only force that can suppress this neo-barbarism and replace it with something better.

Quick, seemingly miraculous, transformations in the thinking of labour movements have occurred and will occur. That worker who accepts capitalism is in a condition in which her objective interests as both worker and human being are at odds with the ideas about society and the world she has been taught to accept. Once that begins to change, everything can change.

Marxism is a necessary part of this process. Labour movements can arrive at vaguely "socialist" hopes and aspirations, just as young people can arrive at angry rebellion against capitalism. Scientific understanding of capitalism, of society, of the centrality of the working class and the politics of working class self-liberation — in short, understanding of how we can map the way from capitalism neo-barbarism to human liberation — does not arise "spontaneously". That is what Marxist theory is for. That is Marxism's irreplaceable contribution.

Writing about Russia 100 years ago, Lenin put it like this: "Social-Democracy [the revolutionary Marxist movement] is a combination of the labour movement with socialism. Its task is not passively to serve the labour movement at each of its separate stages, but to represent the interests of the movement as a whole, to point out to this movement its ultimate aims and its political tasks, and to protect its political and ideological independence. Isolated from Social-Democracy, the labour movement becomes petty and inevitably becomes bourgeois: in conducting only the economic struggle, the working class loses its political independence; it becomes the tail of other parties and runs counter to the great slogan: 'The emancipation of the workers must be the task of the workers themselves'.

"In every country there has been a period in which the labour movement existed separately from the socialist movement, each going its own road; and in every country this state of isolation weakened both the socialist movement and the labour movement. Only the combination of socialism with the labour movement in each country created a durable basis for both the one and the other. But in each country this combination of socialism with the labour movement took place historically, was brought about in a special way, in accordance with the conditions prevailing at the time in each country. The process of combining the two movements is an extremely difficult one, and there is therefore nothing surprising in the fact that it is accompanied by vacillations and doubts."

And again: "The strikes of the 1890s [in Russia] revealed far greater flashes of consciousness: definite demands were put forward, the time to strike was carefully chosen, known cases and examples in other places were discussed, etc. While the earlier riots were simply uprisings of the oppressed, the systematic strikes represented the class struggle in embryo, but only in embryo.

"Taken by themselves, these strikes were simply trade union struggles, but not yet Social-Democratic struggles. They testified to the awakening antagonisms between workers and employers, but the workers were not and could not be conscious of the irreconcilable antagonism of their interests to the whole of the modern political and social system, i.e., it was not yet Social-Democratic consciousness. In this sense, the strikes of the 1890s, in spite of the enormous progress they represented as compared with the 'riots', represented a purely spontaneous movement.

"We said that there could not yet be Social-Democratic consciousness among the workers. This consciousness could only be brought to them from without. The history of all countries shows that the working class, exclusively by its own efforts, is able to develop only trade union consciousness, i.e., it may itself realise the necessity for combining in unions, for fighting against the employers and for striving to compel the government to pass necessary labour legislation, etc. The theory of socialism, however, grew out of the philosophic, historical and economic theories that were elaborated by the educated representatives of the propertied classes, the intellectuals. According to their social status, the founders of modern scientific socialism, Marx and Engels, themselves belonged to the bourgeois intelligentsia. Similarly, in Russia, the theoretical doctrine of Social-Democracy arose quite independently of the spontaneous growth of the labour movement; it arose as a natural and inevitable outcome of the development of ideas among the revolutionary socialist intelligentsia."

Today, Marxism, scientific socialism — what in Lenin's time was called Social Democracy — is everywhere separate from the labour movement, greatly more so than when Lenin was writing. To unite Marxism with the labour movement is the task of revolutionary socialists and consistent democrats everywhere. The collapse of Stalinism gives us a better chance of doing that then we have had in 90 years.

But Marxism itself — the consciousness of the unconscious processes of society — Marxism as a guide to revolutionary action, has suffered tremendous blows in the last historical period. The supreme irony is that the collapse of Russian Stalinism, which had through much of the 20th century turned "Marxism" into the pidgin religion of a totalitarian state, should have as its first consequence the discrediting of "Marxism". That is only the first consequence. The collapse of the Russian state-fostered pidgin Marxism clears the way for the development of unfalsified Marxism. We have a considerable way to go yet to achieve that.

Renewing Marxism

The revolutionary Marxist tradition is "given", but Marxism is not. Marxism as a living force in socialist organisations and in the labour movement is not something given — it has to be fought for and won and then again fought for and won over again, and then yet again.

It has to be clarified and refined and augmented, again and again in a never-ending process. That process is, in a word, "the class struggle on the ideological front".

Lenin said it plainly and truly: "Without revolutionary theory there can be no revolutionary movement." He also argued that practice without theory is blind: theory without practice is sterile. In a declaration of the Editorial Board of the revolutionary newspaper *Iskra*, Lenin wrote:

"The intellectual unity of Russian Social-Democrats has still be to established, and in order to achieve this it is necessary, in our opinion, to have an open and thorough discussion of the fundamental principles and tactical questions. Before we can unite, and in order that we may unite, we must first of all firmly and definitely draw the lines of demarcation. Otherwise, our unity will be merely a fictitious unity, which will conceal the prevailing confusion and prevent its complete elimination. Naturally, therefore, we do not intend to utilise our publication merely as a storehouse for various views. On the contrary, we shall conduct it along the lines of a strictly defined tendency. This tendency can be expressed by the word Marxism, and there is hardly need to add that we stand for the consistent development of the ideas of Marx and Engels, and utterly reject the half-way, vague and opportunistic emendations which have now become so fashionable".

Having rejected eclecticism and indifferentism, he went on:

"But while discussing all questions from our own definite point of view, we shall not rule out of our columns polemics between comrades. Open polemics within the sight and hearing of all Russian Social-Democrats and class conscious workers are necessary and desirable, in order to explain the profound differences that exist, to obtain a comprehensive discussion of disputed questions, and to combat the extremes into which the representatives, not only of various views, but also of various localities or various 'crafts' in the revolutionary movement inevitably fall. As has already been stated, we also consider one of the drawbacks of the present-day movement to be the absence of open polemics among those holding avowedly differing views, an effort to conceal the differences that exist over extremely serious questions."

These words offer a guide to revolutionary Marxists now. They will guide the conduct of the Alliance for Workers' Liberty. The fight for Marxism and for a Marxist labour movement is the fight to prepare the only force capable of taking humanity out of our age of neo-barbarism, the working class, for that task. It is for that task that the Alliance for Workers Liberty exists and fights.

Sixty issues of the Workers' Liberty magazine, in tabloid format, at bit.ly/workersliberty

CLASS AGAINST CLASS
THE MINERS' STRIKE 1984-5

HOW SOLIDARITY CAN CHANGE THE WORLD
A handbook of socialist politics
Articles by Frederick Engels, Karl Kautsky, Rosa Luxemburg and Leon Trotsky

Capital
Karl Marx
Abridged by Otto Rühle

GRAMSCI IN CONTEXT
Essays and interviews
Edited by Martin Thomas

The Fate of the Russian Revolution
Lost Texts of Critical Marxism Vol 1

The Fate of the Russian Revolution volume 2
The two Trotskyisms confront Stalinism

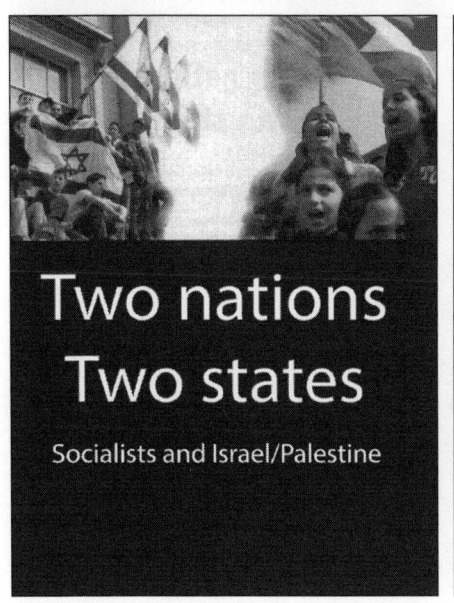

Two nations Two states
Socialists and Israel/Palestine

THE RUSSIAN REVOLUTION: WHEN WORKERS TOOK POWER
PAUL VERNADSKY

The first edition of this book — Can Socialism Make Sense, 400 pages with many supplementary texts — is available from www.workersliberty.org/books